THE PARAFLIGHT EXPERIENCE

THE PARAFLIGHT EXPERIENCE

JOHN RICHARD CARR

WALTZ
PUBLISHING

First Edition
Copyright © 1991 by John Richard Carr

Library of Congress Catalog Card Number: 91-90953
ISBN 0-9629429-6-0

Book design by Crane Duplicating Service Inc.

PUBLISHED BY:
Waltz Publishing
P. O. Box 6088
Fall River, Massachusetts 02724

Printed in the United States of America.

**The true story
of one man's adventure
into the exotic world
of personal flight.**

"The Paraflight Experience"
is a tribute to the safest form
of recreational flying ever
devised by man.
The incredible
POWERED PARACHUTE!

CONTENTS

ACKNOWLEDGMENTS

Special thanks to all of the people who supported my efforts.

In alphabetical order they are:

Walter J. Burns Jr., Alice E. Carr, Walter R. Carr, Michael Champagne, Anne M. Cole, John S. Cole, John A. DePippo, Thelma (King) Dzialo, Thomas Riley, David W. Smith.

Photos were taken by the author and Photographer Tom Dzialo.

Thanks to ParaPlane® Corporation and Steve Snyder for the use of the ParaPlane® parts layout drawing.

"ParaPlane"® is the registered trademark of ParaPlane® Corporation's make of powered parachute ultralight aircraft.

Disclaimer

The author and publisher wish to make clear that flying a powered parachute without full and proper training by authorized personnel, should never be attempted. All flying experiences described in this publication utilize the ParaPlane model powered parachute. Other makes may or may not be similar.

The purpose of this book is to inform and entertain. Application of information or procedures derived from this book is not within control of the author, therefore, liability for use of this information is hereby disclaimed by the author and publisher.

This book is dedicated

to my mother

Gladys M. Carr

"..... I feel like a kite
dancing in the air;
like I'm going places
but I don't know where;
and I'm catching
all these currents
going up and down;
rising and falling
all over this town ....."

from the song: "Kites"

by Barb Schloff

INTRODUCTION

Have you ever wished you could fly? Have you ever wanted to view the world from an entirely new perspective? Think about it. I'm not talking about flying in a conventional airplane. I'm talking about seat of the pants flying. Imagine being hauled into the air as if you were sitting in a lawn chair and something scooped you off the ground, pulled you up to a thousand feet and let you see the world as you never saw it before! It's an experience you wouldn't soon forget. It was my dream ever since I could remember.

When I was a child, I used to enjoy flying a kite. I would stand in an open field for hours and imagine what it would be like to be up there on that kite looking down at the ground. How wonderful it would be to see the area I grew up in from up above. To be up on that kite looking down upon the whole neighborhood. How I wished it could be so.

These thoughts occupied my mind quite often back then, and even as I grew older, I always remembered those early desires for flight. Then, one evening about six years ago as I was watching a TV show, I saw what I knew would be the realization of my dream.

They called it a ParaPlane! These people were sitting in a little three wheeled cart and being hauled off into the air by a giant parachute! The way I saw it they were literally flying a kite! Flying one as I had always imagined. From that day on, I knew my life would never be the same.

The last six years have been filled with an amazing series of learning experiences for me. Just about every fantasy I had regarding personal flight has been realized. What started out as extreme trepidation turned into supreme confidence. You see, although I always wanted to fly, I had a strong fear of heights. Never in my wildest dreams did I really think I could overcome this fear, but as you will see my fantasies truly became a reality. That is what this book is all about. Over these pages I will take you on a very real adventure. You will share in the most exciting phases of flying a powered parachute derived from over four hundred magical flights. You will meet the inventor of the ParaPlane, Steve Snyder, a colorful character and a world renowned aeronautical engineer. But most of all, you will know what it's really like to fly a ParaPlane, how its done, what can and can't happen, and the true fact that anyone, even you, can now safely experience this phenomenal natural high.

CHAPTER 1

CASTLES IN THE AIR

Fasten your seat belts, ladies and gentlemen! You are about to embark on a wondrous adventure that truly has no rival. The following scenario is a fascinating compilation of the most enjoyable moments I have experienced in over four hundred dramatic flights. All of the events are factual with no exaggerations. I've consolidated them into two unique para-flight experiences, and **you** are the pilot!

Your day begins on a warm Indian summer morning in southern New England. Outside of your open bedroom window the melodic sound of songbirds fills the air. For some reason, you feel exceptionally good this morning. You rise and gaze out the window. The autumn leaves have reached their peak colors, and they radiate their brilliance even in the faint light of dawn.

The sky is clear except for a few puffy white fair weather clouds. The wind is dead calm. You have the time, and you know this would be a perfect day to fly your powered parachute ultralight airplane. After a number of preliminary flights, you now feel confident in your abilities as a pilot of this category of aircraft. You are no longer nervous and uncertain. In fact, you can't wait to get started.

Arriving at the field you will fly out of, you check the wind sock for direction, and select an appropriate launch area. The sun has not yet risen, and the grass shimmers from a blanket of dew. After removing the tie downs, you lift your ParaPlane from its trailer, and begin your pre-flight routine. Starting at the front, you work your way around the aircraft.

Tires are properly inflated and free turning. Cables are secure and not frayed. Steering lines are in good shape and properly routed. All necessary pins are in place. All hardware is secure. Propellers are free of nicks along the leading edge. Fuel lines free of leaks. Drive belts are tight.

To be sure you haven't missed anything, you check your pre-flight card. When you are ultimately convinced that all is well, you lift the parachute from the seat and place it on top of the airframe. Walking around back, you place the chute on the ground behind the craft, keeping it in the same orientation as in the seat. The braided lines unfurl as you pull the chute back and slip the storage bag off. You fold the bag and store it in a pocket behind the seat. Starting at the cart, you run your fingers along the lines to the chute, making sure there are no tangles, and checking their integrity. Everything is found to be proper.

You've completed your pre-flight and are now ready to fly. You put in your ear plugs, and don your helmet. With your leg against the seat, you pull start both engines. The chute (wing) comes to life, flopping up and down in the prop wash. Sitting in the seat, with one foot against the front wheel to prevent the cart from rolling, you fasten your seat belt and adjust it for a snug fit.

While the engines are warming up, you begin to get an adrenalin rush. Soon the limited perspective you now have will open up, and you will see the world you live in from a God-like stance. Although you're wearing ear plugs to dampen the engine noise, you know you won't miss your sense of hearing. It will only serve to heighten your other senses.

It has been about twenty minutes since you arrived at the field. The morning sun is about to peek over the horizon. You make a last minute check for other planes in the area, then look back at your chute. When the leading edge of the waving chute is on the upswing, you position your feet on the steering arms, and add some throttle. The cart begins to roll forward, and the chute rises overhead. To completely inflate a folded section of your developing wing, you push both steering arms forward and release them. The stubborn cells pop open, and your wing centers itself above the cart. A little more throttle, a slight course correction, and you're ready for liftoff.

With a slow deliberate push, you advance the throttle to its full forward position. The bumpy ride that you are experiencing over the uneven grass field suddenly becomes smooth, as the craft gently lifts off the ground. You have rolled only sixty feet from your starting position, and now you are climbing into the sky at about four hundred feet a minute.

A gentle breeze on your face tells you that you are moving, but as your altitude increases, the sensation is one of hovering. The ground shrinks in size below you, as more and more scenery comes into view. You feel the air getting cooler as you rise.

At six hundred feet, you level off and kick the right steering arm to line up with the rising sun. Golden rays of sunlight streak across the horizon, brightly illuminating just the tips of the taller multi-colored trees. The heavily forested landscape takes on a surreal glow. It appears as if someone has strung millions of Christmas tree lights throughout the woods. No Hollywood special effects team could ever duplicate this scene!

You feel as though you are on a magic carpet ride. When you look straight ahead, it's easy to imagine that you're just floating in the air with no visible means of support. It seems like a dream, but you know that it's real. Very, very real. You feel as though you are a piece of the earth that has broken away, and gone aloft to take a look at the rest of itself. You are part of what you see, and what you see is beautiful beyond description.

During your few minutes of euphoria, you have increased your altitude without realizing it. The altimeter now reads twelve hundred feet. Leveling off, you check your previously full fuel tank, and find that it's still almost full. The day is young, and you have about an hours worth of fuel left.

Visibility on this day is almost unlimited. You break your transfixed eyes away from the best "scenic overlook" you have ever seen, and look upward. Bright white clouds of various shapes and sizes float overhead. Out of the blue, you feel an uncontrollable urge to visit one. Why Not? You know you can. After all, you're halfway there already.

The little cart swings forward as you push the throttle to climb. Within minutes, you're up to 2800 feet, and watching the clouds float by on both sides of you. Directly in front of you, is a very dense snow white cloud, about 200 feet in diameter. You've never been this close to a real cloud -- at least not out in the open air. What would it be like to fly through it? It's small enough -- you shouldn't be in it long -- you have to find out.

Making slight course corrections, you line the craft up to punch through the center. The air is cool and crisp at this altitude, and your teeth begin to chatter. One last look at the world below, and you're facing a wall of white. Forty feet to go -- thirty feet -- ten feet -- here goes!

Instantly, all visibility is erased. Everything is so intensely white, your eyes hurt. You can't even see your feet in front of you. Water droplets condense on your face. Dampness surrounds you. For a few seconds you become disoriented, but you know you are flying level, and in about twenty seconds you will exit the cloud.

You take a deep breath and are amazed by the aroma. This puffy white cloud has a faintly sweet fragrance. You breathe deeply. The scent is fresh and clean, and you take multiple deep whiffs to savor the delicate bouquet.

The solitude of this pure white environment captivates you. Because you have nothing to reference to, all sense of being high in the sky is temporarily eliminated. The interior of the cloud has washed away any lingering fear of heights you may have harbored. But that secure and peaceful feeling is short lived.

Suddenly, with a flashing rush of thinning white vapor, you are ejected back into the visible world. The abrupt view of the earth, thousands of feet below, shocks you back to reality. You are instantly reminded that your cockpit is little more than a lawn chair! For a brief moment, you feel very alone, very vulnerable and very scared. Another cloud looms in front of you, and although you're tempted to enter it, you decide that you've had enough of this dizzying height and numbing cold.

The cloud experience has been fascinating, and you vow that the future will hold another visitation. You pull the throttle back to idle, and the ParaPlane begins its normal slow descent. Since you cannot descend rapidly (normal power off drop rate is only about 7 m.p.h.), you utilize the time to observe your surroundings. With the exceptional visibility, you are astounded by what you can see from 2000 feet up in the sky.

The Boston skyline stands out sharply, over fifty miles away. You can see the majestic White Mountains of New Hampshire, which are over one hundred miles away! Almost the entire coastline of New England is vividly displayed for your viewing pleasure. Many thousands of tiny lakes and streams glisten in the early morning sun, like a huge natural mosaic.

Dawn from your bedroom window was never like this.

As your altitude decreases, distant views become obscure. You begin to focus your eyes on an exposed patch of ground, in the middle of a heavily forested area directly below you. It looks like it might make a good landing spot in case of an emergency, so you decide to check it out. The altimeter reads 400 feet now, and the cool air is warming up. To facilitate a quicker descent, you initiate a full right turn, and spiral down, enjoying the twirling "carnival like" ride as you go.

From higher altitudes, the field looked smooth and clear, but as you get closer, the surface is not as it appeared. You level off a few feet above the grass, and you can see many large rocks and thick bushes. As you fly along the field, some areas are clear enough to land on, but only in case of emergency.

The field tapers near the end, and becomes a long, thin corridor, surrounded on both sides by tall orange and gold trees. It seems to go on for miles, so you follow it for a while, flying under the tree line to sharpen your low flying skills. Along the pathway, you begin to imagine yourself as an ancient warrior riding his chariot down some medieval concourse. The low trees become adversaries, and you swerve to avoid them. The colonnade begins to narrow, so you take to the sky like an ancient greek deity returning to the heavens. Flying fantasies feature fanciful fun!

The time has come to return to the airfield to avoid running out of fuel. You're cruising at 500 feet and decide to fly over a narrow section of the river. Looking straight down, it's possible to discern all the shallow areas from the deep areas of water, due to the different shades of color. The calm waters allow you to actually see the channel that is dredged down the middle of the river for large ships to pass.

Along the shoreline below you, numerous flitting sea birds weave back and forth in a manner that implies they symbolically acknowledge your presence. It feels as though they sense that you have something in common with them as you share the glorious wonders of personal flight. Until now, you've never really appreciated the special relationship birds have with the environment. They enjoy a distinctive type of freedom, a unique oneness with the marvels of nature. A warm feeling of kinship with all of your fine feathered friends comes over you as you begin to understand their extraordinary lifestyle.

Out on the horizon, the deepening blue of the river water merges into the vast powder blue sky. The forest slowly desolves into city streets and neatly arranged houses. Long shadows like reaching fingers stretch out from the multitude of homes, linking them together like a huge black net. It is only early morning.

The field you took off from comes into view. Although you have been flying for little more than an hour, the duration seems longer because of your heightened senses and many remarkable experiences.

As you near the field in your tiny canvas seat, you look down to the left of your kneecap and spot a white tail deer, two hundred feet below, curiously examining your car and trailer. With the throttle at idle, you float to within fifty feet of the deer before he spots you and turns tail.

The air is so calm that you are able to level off just inches above the ground and fly the length of the field, brushing the tips of the taller grass, like a landspeeder out of the movie "Star Wars". After a quick fly around, you again level off close to the ground and with a gentle pull, bring the throttle back and softly touch down alongside your car.

This exceptionally enjoyable flight leaves you feeling elated and alive, and very hungry. Within fifteen minutes, you've packed up, secured the winsome ParaPlane on its trailer, and are heading down the road to a diner for breakfast. Along the way, a graceful white sea gull glides overhead, banks sharply and hovers for a while, then drifts toward the seashore. You find yourself smiling. You know first hand what he is experiencing. You've been there.

At the diner, as you proceed to gobble up your breakfast, patrons stare at your ParaPlane in the parking lot. You overhear the usual questions.

"It has propellors, but where are the wings?"

"It must be some kind of an air boat."

You wonder what they would think if they knew that only an hour ago, you were sitting in the thing and dangling thousands of feet in the air. A curious patron inquires, and you reveal to him an abbreviated version of your flight. The look on his face tells you that although he professes to believe you, he thinks you are lying through your teeth. It's hard for the average person with no knowledge of ultralight aircraft to comprehend the reality of flying in such a flimsy looking aircraft. The thing just doesn't look like an airplane. No matter though. If weather permits, you know you will be back in the sky by late afternoon.

The entire day turns out to be just as calm as the morning. While completing your planned tasks, you wish you could take advantage of a rare opportunity and fly all day. Nevertheless, soon you are heading back to the field with your ParaPlane in tow, for another flight before sundown.

The western skyline is layered with long strips of high puffy clouds, drenched in pink, hinting at the possibility of a magnificent sunset. You have an hour of daylight left when you reach the field.

Twenty minutes after your arrival, you're snugly strapped into the spartan black seat that will soon become your aerial viewing platform. The ground in front of you is sporadically covered with lumpy tufts of grass that will bounce you around, but only for a few feet until you gently lift off.

A quick twist of your head confirms that your chute is ready for flight. Your gloved hand advances the throttle to full, initiating your transition into the third dimension. Within seconds, you're climbing smoothly into the late afternoon sky.

The pink clouds you had witnessed earlier have evolved into bright red puffs of cotton, blanketing the horizon. Reaching 800 feet, you stop climbing and set the throttle for level flight. The wind speed at this altitude matches your flying speed, allowing you to hover in one spot. The setting sun is brilliantly displayed before you, revealing itself in glowing thin strips behind wisps of misty vapor. The spectacle is awesome. Crimson clouds roll and dance as if expertly choreographed. Orange beams radiate out in every direction from the earth's gradually eclipsing star.

You loosen your seat belt. You cross your legs. You sit back and relax in your 800 foot high theater seat. Nature is staging an alluring exhibition of grand proportions, and you've got the best seat in the house. No one is jabbering away behind you, disturbing your train of thought. No one is sitting in front of you, blocking your view. For once, it doesn't matter how short or tall you are. Nothing can obscure your view. In fact, when you think about it, this show is a command performance, orchestrated especially for you! You are the special guest of honor.

The show lasts about twenty minutes, and when it is over, you find your hands clapping. It's the least you can do for such a magnificent display. Besides, someone up there just might be listening, so you feel compelled to show your approval with an energetic round of applause.

The sun has set. That fabulous purveyor of warmth has left the stage, closing the show with a graying silver curtain of approaching darkness. Below you, street lights and headlights come to life, while above you the sun's companions begin to penetrate the twilight. As much as you would like to continue the adventure, soon it will be dark, so you ease back on the throttle, and initiate your descent.

At 600 feet, you break out of the stronger upper level winds, and begin to move forward. The evening calm has arrived, and the air is very still. For the fun of it, you decide to spiral down. A little more throttle, a full deflection right turn, and your little aircraft becomes an amusement park ride. Banked thirty degrees and spinning in circles, you are afforded an incredible 360 degree panorama. Snake-like streams, checkered fields, and rows of impeccably dressed houses blend together to form a surreal modern art painting, as you spin steadily toward the earth below.

At 200 feet, you release your foot pressure on the right steering arm, and the cart settles down and assumes its normal position under the wing. Your landing field is now in front of you. Easy throttle adjustments are all that are necessary, to set down precisely within a few feet of your car.

As your diminutive aircraft settles down upon the grass, the shimmering blanket of dew that greeted you at dawn has reappeared in the twilight, magically ending a fabulous day of flying. A tremendous amount of exhilaration and enjoyment was afforded you, and all for a few dollars worth of gasoline and two cycle oil.

So there you have it; my compendium of scenic soaring. With over four hundred ParaPlane flights to draw experiences from, it's quite impossible to put everything into one day of flying. These two flights only scratch the surface, but I hope I have given you some idea of the incredible satisfaction you can derive from "Seat of the pants flying".

Although I am now confident of my abilities as a powered parachute pilot, it hasn't always been that way. Six years ago, I knew very little about flying, but like most people, I secretly wanted to fly. Also, like many people, height terrified me.

In dreams, with my arms outstretched, I would personally soar above the countryside. Then without warning, I would lose my ability to fly, and tumble helplessly toward the ground, screaming and waking up in a cold sweat, thankful that it was only a dream.

CHAPTER 2

AWAKENING THE DREAM

Winter was fast approaching. It was that time of year when most of us New Englanders settle in for a period of hibernation. I was avidly looking forward to conjuring up some sort of project to occupy the winter season. Late in November of 1983, viewing a TV show called "Evening Magazine," I watched intently as a segment on a new type of Ultralight Aircraft was being shown. I scrambled up to my Video Cassette Recorder and popped in a blank tape just in time to catch the last two thirds of the broadcast. After the show had concluded, I played the tape over and over, totally fascinated with the unique capabilities of this strange little aircraft.

They called it a "ParaPlane." From what I could perceive, it was basically a powered parachute.

"What could be safer?" I reasoned. "If you lost power, you come down on a parachute. Your parachute is always open! It's opened up before you leave the ground, and until you land. In addition to being your wing, it is also a fully operational recovery system. What could be safer? My God! You could literally pass out in this thing, and it will let you down easy! This has got to be the answer to my dreams."

I was rationalizing the safety of the craft with good reason. For as long as I could remember, I had a very real fear of heights. This probably originated in my childhood days. My friends and I used to climb tall trees and jump off of fairly high places. We would jump from higher and higher points, competing to see who could jump down the furthest distance. Even though our feet would sting severely on impact with the hard ground, we would continue to climb higher to prove we could do it. This foolish childhood game went on for some time in those early years.

One day, we had climbed a particularly high abandoned building. It was my turn to jump, and I sat on the edge of the roof trying to get the nerve to take the plunge. No one that I knew of had ever jumped from this height. I sat there for the longest time, and no matter how hard I tried, I just could not get myself to jump. The distance was just too great. I had lost my confidence and the fear of heights had begun to take root in my subconscious mind. Another reinforcement of this fear was due to friends (and I use the term loosely) occasionally pretending to push you off the edge before you were ready to jump. Fears that occur at this young an age have a way of staying with you. So it was with me. Standing at the edge of a tall building would petrify me. If I were up on a roof, I could not let go of a handhold long enough to do any effective work.

By now, I'm sure you see my point. However, I don't believe "fear of heights" is the real culprit. I believe it's really fear of falling! You know in your mind that if you fall from high enough, it's all over. You've bought the farm. So whether it's fear of heights, fear of falling, or fear of death, the end result is the same.

Because of our fears, we often tend to put off doing a lot of things we really like. My fascination with flying also started at an early age. Although my teens were filled with cars and racing, I secretly always wanted to fly. I envied the birds and other flying creatures. It seemed to me that they had such an advantage over man. Perhaps they lack our gift of intelligence, but they were born with some capabilities far exceeding ours. At their whim, they can take to the skies and soar over forests and rivers, and see the grandeur of nature in a personal way that we can only dream about. Until now.

Over the next few weeks, I found out all that I could about the ParaPlane. Fortunately, I met someone who told me that "Popular Mechanics" magazine had done an article on the Para-Plane. This article answered some of my questions, but I still had more. I mailed to the company for their info package. More weeks passed. Finally, I was convinced that this was the way for me to fly. Everything about it seemed incredibly safe. I called the company and placed my order for a ParaPlane. They informed me that the craft could not be sent directly to me. It would have to be sent to the nearest dealer. There, I would be required to take a first flight course, which included flying on the same day! Casting my fears aside, I placed my order.

The nearest dealership turned out to be next to a little town on the border of Massachusetts and New Hampshire. I waited a month...two months...still no ParaPlane. The dealer was to call me upon arrival. By now, I was getting quite anxious, so I called the company. They informed that the reason for the delay was the canopy I had ordered. It was to be red, white, and blue. (I thought it would be patriotic.) Multi colored canopies take longer to produce. They are special orders. After some thought, I decided to go with a standard canopy in order to save time.

"What colors can you ship right away?" I said.

"Black and Blue" was the reply.

"Who would want black and blue?" I asked.

"It's the only color available at this time."

"Well...OK ship it! What the hell, maybe it will be a good omen." I replied.

I couldn't believe I did this. I ordered a black and blue canopy! Not that I'm superstitious, mind you, but why take any chance? I imagined myself in a body cast. A nervous feeling was coming over me. I didn't really know if I could go through with this.

"What if I were to panic on my first flight?" I thought. "What if I froze up at the controls? What if...wait a minute! If I keep thinking negatively I'll never go through with it. Come on, wake up and smell the coffee, John. This is your dream. This is exactly what you have been waiting for. You can't chicken out this soon. Come on, get with the program! Don't be such a wimp!"

I tried every cliche' in the book to convince myself, but I was still very nervous.

It was now early May, 1984. The winter chill was fast becoming a memory. My ParaPlane, which I had already bought and paid for, was sitting in a hanger about one hundred miles north of my home.

Located in Pepperell, Mass., the dealership is known as "Flight Innovations, Inc." The two men who run the operations, Steve Kalvelage and Rick Sentner, informed me that unless the weather was quite calm, no first time pilots would be allowed to fly. I was to be notified as soon as wind conditions were acceptable. They seemed genuinely concerned about making the first flight an enjoyable experience. I liked the fact that they seemed well schooled on ParaPlane flights. I was beginning to feel more secure. Still, I had never seen an actual ParaPlane up close and personal.

Due to the fact that I work full time, I had asked Steve and Rick to schedule my first flight for a weekend. Two weekends passed, and still the weather would not cooperate. It seemed every weekend was either too windy or too rainy. Although I was getting impatient, I felt very strongly that conditions would have to be perfect or I probably would never go through with this. I decided to use my time furthering my knowledge of the ParaPlane. You can never know too much about a subject, so I rummaged through all of my pamphlets to go over the questions and answers once again. Everything I read seemed repetitious, but I wanted to be sure that I didn't forget anything. Steve had told me that my ParaPlane had been shipped without the owners manual. It was back ordered. Since I had to wait so long to fly, I thought the manual would have been really beneficial. The information that I had available would have to suffice.

Friends of mine were beginning to show some concern. Upon learning about my desire to fly, most of them were somewhat indifferent. However, when they learned that I had actually spent a few thousand dollars on a ParaPlane, their reactions were quite mixed. Some friends thought I was just plain crazy. Reactions ranged from: "You are out of your mind!" and "You would never catch me going up in one of those things!" to "Wow, that seems like it would be a lot of fun!" Of course, knowing how some people look at ultralight flight, I fully expected such remarks and learned to live with them. Some were tolerant and somewhat unruffled, still others were very supportive. These were the people I considered my true friends. I could understand why some people were skeptical. After all, this was a very new type of flying activity. It was possible that some unforeseen circumstances could jeopardize the safety of anyone who participated in this type of flying. I, more than any of my peers, was fully aware of the possible consequences. At times, I even considered calling it quits, but the desire to fly and conquer my fear of heights was very strong indeed. I had waited a long time for this type of opportunity to present itself. There was no way I was going to back out at this point in time.

Two very good friends of mine were my biggest supporters. My cousin John DePippo was one. John and I grew up together in Fall River, Mass. It was during the early years that John affectionately became known as "Pip". Pip backed my decision to do my thing, all the way. Although I could sense he was skeptical from the onset, he had a pretty good idea how I felt about this, and was more than willing to help out. The other person supporting me, was my friend Mike Champagne. He knew my reasons to realize my dream and stuck by me one hundred percent. It was a comfort to have someone to discuss my feelings with. All things considered though, I truly feel that a person has to make his own decisions in life, be they right or wrong.

"I may have all the support I need right now," I reasoned, "but when it comes to flying the ParaPlane for the first time, I will be all alone."

Unlike any other ultralight aircraft, with the ParaPlane, you have to solo on your first flight! No one can go with you, because the ParaPlane can carry only one person. However, you are in contact by radio, with your flight instructors on the ground. Knowing this gave me some reassurance. Although, just the thought of lifting off the ground in a little three wheeled cart, sitting out in the open, would leave me with a very nervous feeling.

It was the middle of May on a cool Thursday evening that I received a call from Steve, one of the instructors at the dealership.

"Looks like this Saturday is going to be a good day to schedule your first flight course, John."

"Great," I said, as a chill ran down my spine.

"Try to arrive early, say, about seven o'clock."

"No problem," I said, trying to sound cool. When I hung up the phone though, my reaction was quite different. "This is it!" I exclaimed, "I'm finally going to do it! It's just one day away." My thoughts were a jumble of mixed emotions and although I tried to calm myself down....the night was sleepless.

Friday, May eighteenth, 1984, was anything but a normal day for me. At work, I found it hard to concentrate. My mind was racing over thoughts of what tomorrow would bring. How would I react? Would I chicken out? What if I panicked? Will the weather hold out?....The day was fraught with a limitless number of mixed feelings, ranging from elation to fear, and lack of sleep has a way of carrying them to the extreme.

The people at work wished me luck, and I arrived home that evening with an extremely strong sense of anticipation. None of my friends were available to accompany me on my venture in the morning. I would have to go it alone. After reading over all of the material I had available on the ParaPlane, I resolved to get a good nights sleep. The previous night encompassed an endless bout of tossing and turning, and I wanted to be sure that tonight was not a repeat performance.

I read some unrelated material, watched some television, and made myself a soothing drink. Then I set my alarm clock for three thirty in the morning to get an early start, and since I was tired and exhausted, I went to bed as early as possible.

It was another sleepless night.

CHAPTER 3

FIRST FLIGHT

Saturday morning arrived in darkness. Since I was awake most of the night anyway, I disabled my alarm before it had a chance to ring. It seemed that any possibility of a good night's sleep would have to wait until my introduction to flying was over. Peering out of my bedroom window into the darkness, I strained my sleepy eyes in an effort to detect any possible breeze. Silhouettes of reaching tree branches were outlined against the faint pre-dawn sky. All was calm. Not a hint of motion could be detected. This was exactly the kind of day I was waiting for.

After fumbling into my clothes, I poured a breakfast of cereal and coffee into an uneasy stomach. It was four thirty in the morning when I finally left the house. The engine on my six year old car creaked and groaned as it came to life, and I headed north on the highway. After an hour into the two hour trip, lack of sleep began to take its toll. Gravity was tugging on my eyelids, so I decided to pull over in a clearing and take a ten minute nap.

Three hours later, a ray of sunshine on my face awakened me. I checked my watch. It was after eight o'clock, and I still had at least an hours drive ahead of me. At this point, I knew my chances of getting to the field early were shot, but the sleep was good, and I felt somewhat rejuvenated. As I accelerated up to highway speed, I noticed the tops of the trees were beginning to sway back and forth. The light breeze at that point should not have alarmed me, but it was only eight thirty, and I knew things could only get worse. Realizing that I couldn't change the time or weather, I resolved to accept things as they were, and just do the best I could under the circumstance.

It was about nine thirty when I arrived at the field under a partly cloudy sky. I was expecting to see ParaPlanes all over the sky, but the place looked deserted. There was a large hanger type building on the property. The field was all grass covered and in need of cutting. I decided to enter the building first, bypassing the office. As I walked through the hangar door, I was taken aback by my first up close look at a ParaPlane! It was a strange looking craft, that seemed much bigger than I had imagined. It looked other worldly. I sat in the little black canvas seat and tried to imagine myself up in the air on board the thing. The thought of it scared the daylights out of me! It was like I was sitting in a lawn chair, with everything wide open around me.

As I was marveling at the simplicity of the craft, a voice startled me. I looked up and saw a rather heavy set man wearing a ParaPlane tee shirt. He introduced himself as Steve, one of the flight school instructors. I told him who I was, and that I was anxious to get started. He introduced me to his partner, Rick. Rick was leaner than Steve, and looked more like a Para-Plane pilot to me, because of his weight. They informed me that none of the ParaPlanes I was looking at were mine. My unit was still in the folded state. This was because they wanted me to know how to fold and unfold it. I knew of the ParaPlane's portability, of course, but I didn't expect this to be a part of the course.

One other person was scheduled to take a first flight course on this Saturday. He was a tall, stocky man named Tim, who lived about a hundred miles further away than I did. Tim and I got acquainted, and set about the task of assembling a Para-Plane. We got no help from Steve and Rick. They felt we would learn better if we did it ourselves.

As we were fumbling through assembling our respective aircraft, we talked of the reasons we wanted to fly. Tim related to me that he had tried sport parachuting, and various other aircraft oriented activities. He seemed very confident and secure with what was to come. I, on the other hand, was a bundle of nerves. I had no desire to jump out of a perfectly good airplane! At least he was no better at assembling a Para-Plane. It was taking both of us an eternity. I wished I had his apparent confidence about flying.

It was supposed to take about twenty minutes to unfold a ParaPlane using no hand tools, but a straight screwdriver. It took us about an hour, not bad, I reasoned, for a couple of rank amateurs. Usually, I'm quite adept at mechanical things, but usually I'm not such a nervous wreck.

After finally unfolding our ParaPlanes, and mounting the engine (power) systems, we were ready for the classroom. This consisted of a verbal discussion on the flying characteristics of the ParaPlane, and procedures to follow in case an emergency situation should arise. We then viewed a video presentation showing an actual ParaPlane first flight. I was quite impressed by the apparent ease at which these "so called" first timers were flying. They looked like professionals to me. Following the video, Tim and I were given a written test, which consisted of all the material we had covered so far. The test was basically simple, and we both had no trouble passing it.

By now, it was the middle of the day, and the inevitable wind had picked up considerably. It was now probably a steady ten miles per hour, and gusting to fifteen. Our instructors assured us that it would most likely calm down later in the day. I had not eaten anything since the morning, and I was beginning to get over anxious, but we weren't ready to fly just yet anyway. Now, it seemed, we were to familiarize ourselves with the intricacies of the parachute. Steve and Rick wheeled my Para-Plane out into the field. Rick unbuckled the chute bag from its resting place in the seat, and handed it over the top of the Para-Plane to Steve. Steve set the bag on the ground, opened the top, and pulled the whole thing back about twenty feet unraveling the braided lines. He dumped the chute out of the bag and spread it out on the ground. At this point, he asked me to turn around and not look until he said to. I was completely puzzled.

"What the hell is he up to?" I wondered. My perplexity was short lived. The purpose of this exercise, I was told, was to show how the chute could get tangled up. When I turned around, the chute looked exactly as he had left it.

"What's the problem?" I asked.

"Do you think it'll fly like that?" Steve asked.

I knew the leading edge of the chute should be on top, so I lifted the center of the canopy to check it out. Sure enough, the chute seemed to be inverted.

"No problem!" I exclaimed.

"Good luck," was the reply.

"Who needs luck?" I asked confidently, as I proceeded to flip the chute over...and over...and over. What a jumbled up mess I made! There are thirty two lines on a seven cell chute, and you would be amazed at how many of them you can entangle. I must have spent an hour trying to figure out what I was doing wrong. Eventually, I solved the puzzle and in so doing, I realized why they let me make such a fool of myself. When you learn something the hard way, you never forget it. It was a long drawn out affair, but I learned that the chute can only really get inverted if you flip it over when lifting it over the craft. It's imperative to pass it over the top in the same position that it sits in the seat. If it does get flipped, you can straighten it out in seconds if you know what you're doing.

Daylight was running out on us, and I was beginning to wonder if we would ever get to fly before sundown. The winds had subsided a bit, and Steve felt it was calm enough now to get a flight in. According to regulations, the instructor flies first, covering the prescribed course exactly the way the student should.

Steve pulled the starter cords on both engines to prime them, then he flipped on the ignition toggle switches. With a single pull on each cord, the little two cycle engines came to life, sputtering and popping like a top fuel dragster. The sound was very loud, but not unpleasant. As Steve was preparing to fly, I was starting to really get cold feet. Swallowing hard, I grit my teeth, and tried hard to convince myself that everything would turn out fine.

Tim and I stood on the sidelines and watched, as Steve buckled the seat belt and edged the throttle forward. The cart started rolling forward through the tall grass, and I watched in awe as the chute billowed out and floated gently up over it. With the chute fully open, Steve pushed the engines to full throttle and within seconds, the craft lifted gently off the ground. The ParaPlane was aloft! (I remember thinking, "At least I know it can fly now".)

It was flying, true, but it was climbing ever so slowly. Soon it became apparent that something was wrong. Steve was gaining no altitude, so he set the ParaPlane down in some tall grass at the end of the field. Rick told us that he must have had a tangled line. Perhaps he was right, but it appeared to me that Steve was just too darn heavy for the ParaPlane to effectively lift up.

Rick, Tim, and I, hopped in a pickup truck, and drove down to where Steve had landed. As we arrived at the end of the field, Steve told us that a line had snagged and he would try again.

We returned to the front of the field, and lifted the Para-Plane off the back of the truck. It wasn't heavy, and two of us had no trouble carrying it. Steve set everything up, pointed the ParaPlane into the wind, and took off again. This time, although his climb was still slow, he gained enough altitude and flew around the prescribed course. He made a perfect easy landing in almost the same spot he took off from. I was very impressed. Now that I had seen it fly, I was a little less apprehensive about doing it myself, although the butterflies in my stomach said otherwise.

The wind was calm now, but the clouds in the sky had thickened, and you could feel an occasional drop of rain. To make matters worse, it was also getting dark. Steve and Rick decided that we had better wait until tomorrow to fly. Part of me was upset that we had to wait, but part of me was very much relieved; I felt dejected at this point, yet, strangely peaceful. Tim and I had learned a lot, but it seemed ironic that we had come so close to a flight, only to have to wait another day. Steve and Rick said they would be at the field by six o'clock; and the weather report was good for tomorrow. Tim decided to stay the night at a nearby motel, since he had such a long drive.

I opted for the two hour ride back to my house. There were two very good reasons for my decision. One, I wanted to get a good night's sleep; two, there was no way the ParaPlane was going to fit in the very small trunk of my car. It's designed to fit in a car trunk, but it has to be a least a mid-sized one.

Pip had told me earlier that he would be free on Sunday if I wanted him to accompany me to the dealership. Since he drove a pickup truck, and I knew the ParaPlane would fit in it, I decided to call him when I got home.

It was eleven o'clock when I arrived home, and I was physically exhausted. It had been a long day. As soon as I got my coat off, I called Pip on the phone. I really hate to call anyone at such a late hour, but this was a special occasion, and Pip is a nighthawk anyway. After hearing about my trials and tribulations of the day, Pip agreed to go with me in the morning. We arranged to meet at his house at five o'clock. I thanked him, hung up the phone, and took a quick shower.

Against all odds, I vowed to get some much needed rest for the few hours remaining.

"Anyone as dog tired as I am should fall asleep immediately," I reasoned. Perhaps I should have, and Lord knows I tried, but what do you think happened?...

You guessed it! Insomnia city.

My mind was racing all night. It seemed that since I really knew what was in store for me now, I was more worried than ever. Nevertheless, it was four in the morning, and I had a mission. I was going to see this dream of mine through, if it killed me. Well, maybe "killed me" is a poor choice of words. How about "If it's the last thing I do." No, that's just as bad. There is no good way to phrase it. It's cut and dry. Either I do it or I don't. That's all there is to it. Cut and dry. No problem. Who am I kidding? I'm a veritable vegetable! I'll never go through with this! I'll never.... The alarm clock rang. It was time to quit dreaming and get the show on the road. I stumbled out of bed, and stuck my head under the cold water faucet. Pip was waiting for me; I was running late. This time I skipped break-fast completely, and ran out of the house. Stopping abruptly, before entering my car, I looked towards the sky and listened intently. It appeared that the weather would be a friend, as no motion could be detected in the shadowy skies. The silence was eerie. You could literally hear a pin drop.

Feeling somewhat relieved, I managed to stay awake on the eight mile drive down to Pip's house. It was a comfort knowing that we were taking his truck, and I would get a chance to rest. When I arrived, Pip was waiting for me with a cup of coffee. He knew I would need it, and he was right.

Shortly thereafter, along with Pip's son Danny, we piled into the pickup and the three of us headed for the highway. On the way up I had thought I would get some sleep, but we all had a lot to talk about, and the opportunity for sleep never arose. At least I didn't have to drive.

As mile after mile rolled by, I watched the tops of the trees for the fluttering signs of wind. There was some motion of the leaves, but not enough to be concerned with. As our arrival time at the field drew closer, a strange feeling of impending doom came over me. It was probably due to the fact that my moment of truth was so close at hand. I knew that I really shouldn't have been worried, after all, I had done my homework, and I had covered every piece of material I owned on the ParaPlane over and over. Why then, was I still a bundle of nerves?

We reached the field at about seven thirty. Pip, Danny and I walked over to the hangar building. Tim had arrived and was waiting inside. Steve and Rick, who were supposed to be there earlier, were nowhere to be found. I introduced Pip and Danny to Tim, then asked him where our instructors were. He replied that he had been there for over an hour and they hadn't arrived yet. It was still early, and the wind was still light, so I wasn't too concerned.

We used the extra time to further acquaint ourselves with the ParaPlane. Before long, Steve and Rick arrived, and we were ready to begin our adventure. Rick was to fly first this time to let us know how the conditions were. As he was setting the ParaPlane up, I noticed that it seemed to be a bit windier now. Rick didn't seem concerned, so I figured it was no big deal.

Unlike yesterday, the wind had opened up the ParaPlane canopy this time and it was hanging above the cart like a big kite. Rick didn't need any assistance and when he was ready to fly, he pushed the throttle forward, and the ParaPlane was airborne in just a few feet. We all marveled at how short the takeoff was.

The ParaPlane was rocking a bit as Rick flew it around the prescribed course. This consisted of staying over the field, and making three rectangular passes at about three hundred feet of altitude. On the second pass, Rick incorporated a full three hundred and sixty degree turn in both right and left directions. Then he made a low pass to simulate landing, and took it back up for the final go-round. By this time, the wind was starting to really pick up out of the north. The ParaPlane was rocking quite a bit, and as Rick flew along the tree line on the south end of the field, a gust seemed to push it sideways over the trees. It appeared he was setting up to land, but the wind speed seemed to equal his flying speed, and he was just hovering over the tree line.

Pip, Danny, Tim, and I stood motionless as we watched Rick dangling over the trees in my ParaPlane. We knew he was trying to advance forward, but the gusting winds wouldn't let him.

Finally, after a minute or so, he was able to come forward and drop down for a landing. Even though it was still windy, Rick made a nice gliding approach and touched down gently. Steve ran over and helped him get the chute down in the wind. After securing the chute, Rick came over to where we were standing. He was visibly shaken. He told Tim and I that there was no way he could let us fly in those conditions. We were visibly relieved. I didn't know about Tim, but after seeing what Rick went through, I was in no hurry to fly.

Our instructors informed us that freak wind conditions such as those we witnessed, were not very common. Although it looked like a bad scene, Rick said he wasn't worried because the ParaPlane was built to withstand the shock of free fall, which it will never see. It all seemed logical to me, but I was still not totally convinced.

Two hours passed, and by twelve o'clock the wind settled down just as mysteriously as it came. This was a very unusual turn of events, since in most cases, once the wind picks up in the morning, it does not calm down until evening. Tim and I had pretty much figured that we weren't going to fly that day, when Steve told us it looked like conditions had improved enough to give it a go. Upon hearing this, my heart was in my mouth, and my legs started shaking. That old feeling of incapacitation was creeping up on me.

I turned to Tim, and asked him if he would like to be the first to try. Since he had some parachuting experience, I thought he would be better suited, and I might learn from his experience.

"Why don't you go first, Tim?"

"Well, I was sort of hoping that you would go first, John."

"But, you're more experienced, I think you should be first."

"No, I would really rather have you go first."

"Come on, Tim, I would feel much better if you did it first."

"Well, I would feel much better if you went first, come on, you can do it!"

"Oh, all right, I'll go first."

I couldn't believe I had said that. I had no intention of being the first one of us to fly, but I felt I should honor the commitment. Now, I wasn't just nervous, I was beginning to feel numb.

With my ParaPlane pointed into the wind, Steve laid the chute (wing) out, and started each engine in turn. As I stood on the side, the sound of the engines had a strange calming effect on me. The engines made a dragster like sound that reminded me of my drag racing days.

Steve and Rick were to be my wing holders. They were to hold the chute on each side, and wait for my thumbs up signal.

Pip, Danny and Tim were standing next to me just a few feet away, with strange smiles on their faces. To them, I must have looked frightened. If only they knew how right their feelings were.

I mustered up every ounce of courage I had left, and sat down in the ParaPlane's little black seat. Steve handed me the helmet, and connected the two-way radio. He told me that on the first flight I would have to do without the ear plugs that are normally worn, in order to hear the radio. I donned the helmet, and Rick tried out the radio to assure that it was functional. His voice was deafening. When I asked him to turn down the volume, he refused, saying that if he did, when I got in the air, I wouldn't hear him over the noise of the engine.

Steve gave me a last minute briefing and told me to go over everything in my mind, to take it slow, there would be no hurry, and to wait until I'm ready. I didn't think I would ever be ready.

My two instructors were holding their respective ends of the chute. Tim was waiting on the sidelines with a concerned look on his face. Pip and Danny, who were standing to my right, had nervousness and doubt etched in their smiles. I tried to convince myself, once again, that everything would turn out fine, but my personal psychotherapy wasn't working.

I put my feet into the wire supports on the steering arms and pushed. They didn't seem to move much. My legs seemed to be too short to effectively steer. I called Steve over and explained to him that I could only push the steering arms a few inches before my legs were straight out. He told me not to worry, that it wasn't necessary to push the arms all the way to steer. Perhaps he was right, but I know I would have felt better if I could have.

My moment of truth was at hand. I was holding the Para-Plane from rolling with my foot on the front wheel. I had only to move my foot and position it on the steering arm, then signal the chute holders that I was ready, and add some throttle with my left hand. My heart was in my mouth.

I couldn't do it. I just could not do it. Every time I thought I had mustered enough courage to give it a go, my hand would not move. I couldn't signal the chute holders that I was ready.

I had to calm myself down somehow. Everything was ready. All pre-flighting was done. Somehow, I had to convince myself I could do it. I double checked the seat belt about a dozen times.

In an effort to relax, I leaned my head back against the aluminum air frame. When the helmet contacted the air frame, the engine vibrations caused it to rattle. My vision became blurred for an instant and I quickly pulled my head forward.

"What is wrong with me?" I thought. *"Why can't I just do it? It's perfectly safe, there's no reason in the world to throw in the*

towel now. Come on, John, you've bought and paid for this thing, you've got to fly it at least once."

Nothing seemed to work. It was probably only a few minutes that I sat there, but it seemed like an hour. Finally, with every bit of reckless abandon I could induce in myself, I made the decision to do it. One last look at my cousin, and I turned to the chute holders and gave them the thumbs up sign.

Slowly, I took my foot from the front wheel, and the cart started rolling forward. I looked straight ahead at the tall grass. I inched the throttle forward to about one half. As the cart picked up ground speed, I was supposed to look in the little convex mirror in front of me, to see that the chute had taken its proper place above the cart. I didn't do it. I completely forgot. Against proper judgment, I reasoned that everything must be okay, or they would tell me on the radio.

Reaching down with my right hand, I grasped the little seat as tightly as I could. No sound came from the radio, so I pushed the throttle full forward.

Within an instant, the engine sputtering became a roar, and the cart lifted off the ground. My grip tightened on the seat, as the earth moved away below me. I was mesmerized. I looked straight ahead, fearful that if I looked straight down, I might panic.

The ParaPlane continued to climb, and the view became more and more spectacular. It was like being on a magic carpet. As scared as I was, I marveled at the breathtaking scenery as well as the smoothness of the ride. Once the craft lifted off, the vibrations were much less noticeable.

Euphoria was beginning to replace the numbness I was experiencing. Before I could become totally entranced, the radio crackled with Rick's voice. He told me to bring the throttle back, I was climbing too high. The altimeter read seven hundred feet. I was not flying the course as prescribed, because

I was so taken by the experience. Gathering my nerve, I pushed the left steering arm, in order to turn back towards the field. Nothing happened.

The ParaPlane wouldn't turn. When they showed me on the ground how hard a push it would take to make a turn I wasn't impressed. After all, I was an experienced bicyclist, my legs were more than strong enough to handle a little problem like steering. With my back against the seat, and the seat belt so tight that it was cutting off my circulation, my legs were too short to push the steering arm. I had to do something quick. There was no way I was going to loosen the seat belt.

First, I brought the throttle back to level off, then, I forced my body under the belt to gain some leg length. It wasn't enough, and I had to remove my feet from the stirrups and push with the ball of my foot to get sufficient extension for a shallow turn.

Now I was turning ever so slowly toward the field. As I flew over the field, with my altitude down to three hundred and fifty feet, I gathered together my thoughts, and resolved to complete the first flight course successfully.

I made the first circuit around without a hitch, although my turns were very wide because of my steering difficulties. On my second pass, Rick had to remind me on the radio to do the "figure eight" which consisted of a full circle turn in both directions.

My turns were super wide, but I made them both nonetheless, and continued around for the low pass run. It could hardly have been called a "low pass", since when I saw the ground coming up at fifty feet, I pushed the throttle forward immediately. I was not overly thrilled with the prospect of having to land the thing.

Ready or not, I was on my last go-round and what goes up must come down. My stiff right hand was still securely frozen to the seat, and my left hand had never left the throttle, so when people on the ground waved, there wasn't any way I could wave back. Also, I couldn't use the radio to talk back since this would have required a free hand, and I had none to spare.

Turning on to the downwind leg, I began my final approach to land. At twenty feet or so, I added some throttle to level off. My instructors were out in the field, and I wanted to land near them, to make a good impression. (Hopefully, not an impression in the ground.) The ParaPlane was coming in better than I expected, smooth and slow. As the wheels touched the ground in the high grass, I chopped the throttle all the way back to kill the engines.

I was on the ground, but before I rolled to a stop, I felt a hard bump, and the ParaPlane bounced back into the air. Suddenly, I was drenched with muddy water, and back on the ground. Hidden in the tall grass, was an old rubber tire. I hit the thing dead center and it flipped over and lifted the Para-Plane up, covering me with the slimy water inside it. No harm was done, except for my pride, since I wanted to make a perfect landing.

Safely on the ground, I quickly unbuckled the seat belt, stood up and let out a primal scream. "What an unbelievable experience!" I exclaimed, as I greeted Steve and Rick. They told me I had done well, and I had passed the course. My feeling of accomplishment was so intense, I was grinning from ear to ear.

Pip, Danny, and Tim came running down to where I had landed and greeted me.

"I can't believe you did it, John"! Pip said. "While Danny and I were waiting for you to make a move, we were saying to each other, 'He's not going to do it, I know he's not going to do it,' but then all of a sudden you took off! It was fantastic!"

Pip didn't know how close I really came to not doing it. About every bit of courage I could muster was necessary to pull it off, but the elation I was feeling now, was more than worth the few minutes of agony earlier. I had finally realized my dream!

Tim was very excited, and asked me what it was like, how I felt, and would I do it again. I told him that I couldn't lie to him, I was petrified at the beginning, but as the flight went on, I began to slowly develop more and more confidence. "Now that I've done it, and I know what it's like, I would do it again in a minute!" I said brazenly. "Go over everything in your mind, and when you feel you're ready, just do it!"

Now that it was over for me, I was bristling with confidence, and it showed. But Tim was still nervous, I could sense it. It was his turn now, and I knew from my own experience that nothing anybody says to you will convince you. It's a decision that you have to make alone, no one can make it for you.

We pushed my ParaPlane back to the front of the field. It was nice to relax and just watch as Steve and Rick set up Tim's ParaPlane. Before long, they were ready and Tim buckled himself in. This time, they recruited me to help Steve as a chute holder so Rick could go out in the field with the radio for a better position. After briefing me on holding the chute, Steve told Tim to give us the thumb's up sign when he was ready to go. I kept a sharp eye on Tim. I wanted to make sure everything went well for him.

Suddenly, Tim signaled us and went to half throttle. I looked over at Steve and he nodded, so I let go of the chute at the same time he did, and it started to billow into the air. Tim had taxied about thirty feet at a less than adequate ground speed to fully inflate the chute. With the chute still only half inflated, Tim went to full throttle. He must have done the same thing I did, and not looked in the mirror assuming the chute was open. It was far from open, and the extra thrust at that point seemed to fold the unopened side further under. The lift from the opened side was tipping the cart over. It was on two wheels now, and I could hear Rick from where I was standing, screaming into the radio for Tim to abort the flight. He kept on going at full throttle. Rick, assuming that the radio was not working, started waving the emergency paddles to signal Tim to shut down. He just kept going at full throttle.

Abruptly, the cart, which was now at a forty five degree angle and picking up speed, flipped completely upside down. The propellers, still at full throttle, were digging into the dirt and throwing clumps of sod all over the place.

All of us ran as fast as we could down to the upended Para-Plane. Rick, since he was already out in the field, got there first and quickly pulled the throttle arm back, killing the engines.

Tim was still strapped into the seat, in a fetus like position, upside down. We asked him if he was all right and he didn't respond. He must have been in shock. He appeared to be unhurt, but he wouldn't respond to any questions.

We unbuckled his seat belt, and laid him on the ground next to the cart. After a short time, he came around and Rick asked him why he didn't shut down when he was told to. He had no valid explanation. The only presumption that made any sense was that he must have panicked. Still, he was unhurt except for his pride, and the only thing wrong with the ParaPlane was two badly splintered propellers.

Within a short time, Steve and Rick replaced the props, and gave his ParaPlane a clean bill of health. They asked him if he wanted to give it another try. At this point, he wanted no part of it. He said he wanted to go home and think about it. I didn't blame him one bit.

Watching what had happened to Tim was extremely unsettling to me. Although it was pilot error, and not the fault of the ParaPlane that caused the accident, I quickly felt a strange revelation. It was all too apparent now, that I was fortunate to have been the first to fly. It was so difficult for me to make that first move, that I knew beyond a shadow of a doubt, if I had let Tim go first and saw what happened to him, I never would have flown. Not in a million years.

Pip and Danny gave me a hand folding up the ParaPlane, and we set it down in the bed of the pickup. I received my certificate, said good-bye to everyone, and proudly left the dealership. On the way home, I reflected back on the days activities. Everything on the ground that happened seemed very real indeed to me. But the flying part seemed unreal. It was such a radically new experience for me, that it all seemed like a dream. The reality of it had not really sunk in yet, but the door was opened to a whole new realm of experiences for me.

My dream of conquering my fear of heights and personally flying had finally become a reality. As tired as I was, I still talked incessantly all the way home. I was very proud indeed.

Pip and Danny probably wanted to throw me out of the truck.

CHAPTER 4

THE WINDS OF CHANGE

One full week had gone by since I took my first flight, and I was looking forward, albeit nervously, to my second. During the week, I spent a lot of time extolling the virtues of flying the ParaPlane to just about anybody who would listen. Now the weekend was here, and my anxieties were returning.

Saturday was a windy, cloudy day, and Sunday was sunny, but still quite windy. With my limited experience, I wanted the day to be close to perfect, so a windy day was out of the question for my second flight ever. Just the same, I didn't want to wait too long, for fear I would lose my nerve.

Fortunately, Monday, May 28th, 1984, was a holiday. Weather forecasters were predicting a rain storm but not until mid-day. Even though I knew it would be cloudy in the morning, I figured it would be calm enough, so on Sunday night I made preparations to fly Monday morning.

Since last week, my ParaPlane had been dormant, taking up a small amount of space in a dark recess of my cellar. Knowing it would not fit in my trunk, I called Pip, and asked him if we could use his pickup truck again. He was quite willing, and I told him I was going to get a trailer soon, so he would be off the hook as far as his truck was concerned.

After calling Pip, I telephoned Mike and asked him if he would accompany us in the morning. He had missed my first flight, and was looking forward to seeing the second. He told me he would be there, and he would bring his camera. All the arrangements were made, so it was time to hit the sack for an early rise and shine. Surprisingly, after tossing and turning a while, I slept quite well.

In the morning the sky looked ominous. The weather radio was still saying no rain until noon, and the wind was very light. When Pip arrived, we loaded the ParaPlane into the truck. By eight o'clock, Pip, Danny, Mike, my father and I were at the airport.

Fall River Airport is a small municipal facility on the north end of the city. Before I purchased the ParaPlane, I spoke with the people at the airport, and they assured me it would be acceptable to fly from there. I was counting on this, since there really wasn't any place else nearby to fly from.

There are two runways, a long main runway, and a short cross runway. Along the main runway, which runs basically north-south, is a taxiway on the west side. Between the taxiway and the runway, there are grass strips. Alongside the taxiway to the southwest are numerous parked planes.

Fall River Airport -- Looking Southeast.

Small airports usually have their share of "hangar pilots", people who sit around and talk about flying, and this one is no different. When we quietly announced our arrival, a number of pilots followed us out to the truck to check out the "strange aircraft". I was totally unfamiliar with where to set up at the airport, so I welcomed any suggestions.

Very carefully, I assembled the ParaPlane, making sure everything was done correctly. My nerves were beginning to bother me; I wasn't too crazy about having an audience. This was to be the first time ever I would fly without a radio. I was starting to sweat.

Worry has a way of creeping up on you, and so it was in this situation. My father was worried also. He wouldn't admit it, but I could sense it. As flying time came closer, he appeared to be having some second thoughts about what I had gotten myself into. It was my intent to prove to him that this type of flying was really safe.

Knowing how much trouble I had in steering, I decided to add a boat cushion to the back of the seat, and also to extend the foot rests so I could push the steering arms further. This seemed to be effective.

Since flying off of the grass last week was a bit bumpy, I naturally assumed that flying off of a paved surface would allow for a smoother and easier takeoff. This was also suggested by one of the veteran pilots at the airport. It seemed logical at the time.

Clouds were covering the sky completely by the time I had the ParaPlane ready for flight. Someone had suggested that I try using the taxiway to take off from, thereby leaving the runway free for the planes. Again this sounded logical, so we moved out onto the taxiway.

I briefed Pip and Mike on how to hold the ends of the chute to assist me on takeoff, and asked Danny to hold the front of the craft from moving, so I could start it. The wind was blowing out of the north at about three or four miles per hour. With the front of the ParaPlane pointed straight down the taxiway to the north, I pulled the starter cords on the engines.

Unlike my first flight, the engines did not start on the first pull. It was the first time I tried to start them by myself, and I didn't understand their idiosyncrasies yet.

After a few minutes, I had them running strong. I checked the area for any sign of aircraft coming in, then sat in the seat and buckled up. Three minutes of warm up were required for the engines, so I used the time to try to relax. Looking at the people around me though, made me even more nervous. My father was wearing a very concerned look on his face. All the other observers seemed curiously impassive.

Behind me, Pip and Mike were kneeling on the ground holding the chute. Turning around the best I could against the shoulder harness, I motioned to them that I was ready. Waving

Danny aside, I clenched my teeth, put my feet on the steering arms and added some throttle.

The cart started moving down the taxiway and this time, I looked in the convex mirror to check the chute. There was no chute in the mirror. The cart seemed to be going much faster than the first time, so I couldn't understand why I could not see the chute above me. I added more throttle. The cart was trying to turn every way but the way I was steering.

Only a few feet to the left of me were all the parked planes, and I was getting dangerously close to them. I added still more throttle. Finally, I could see the canopy taking shape in the mirror.

As the chute filled in the mirror, the cart pulled hard to the left, and headed straight for one of the parked planes. At that point I should have aborted the takeoff run, but my adrenaline was flowing, and seeing a full chute, I pushed the throttle full forward. The cart picked up speed, but I was only a few feet from the parked plane and still on the ground! Again, I should have aborted, but instead, I held the throttle as hard forward as I could, said a prayer, and closed my eyes!

Seconds later, I opened my eyes and I was in the air! I couldn't believe it! The feeling of relief was so intense, that I didn't feel nervous, and I let go of the throttle and seat with my hands, waved them in the air, and let out quite a yell.

It was such an incredibly wondrous feeling having made it into the air, but my troubles were far from over. When the ParaPlane reached an altitude of about four hundred feet, I brought the throttle back a bit to level off. The panorama was nothing short of spectacular, and I found myself making many turns in order to take in as much of the scenery as possible.

The seat cushion was a benefit, as I was able to make a full deflection turn now. What I didn't know at the time was that every time you turn the ParaPlane, you lose altitude. This can be compensated for by simply adding a little throttle when you turn, but I wasn't even thinking about that. I was too busy taking in vast areas of the countryside that I had never seen before from this vantage point. Cloudy though it was, I was getting a sense of euphoria from the sheer beauty of the area from up above.

Before I knew it, my altitude was down to about fifty feet, and I was heading straight for a bank of trees on the side of the runway. At the last second, I emerged from cloud nine and realized what was about to happen, so I pushed the throttle to maximum.

For few seconds I continued toward the trees, and it appeared I would hit them, but the ParaPlane rose upward just as I neared the top branches. A rush of adrenaline hit me, and I left the throttle on full until I had gone back up to a few hundred feet.

Just as I was starting to feel somewhat at ease, I felt a few drops of rain hitting me in the face. My glasses were blurred and I had to remove them. Rain was supposed to hold off until noontime, but it was an early forecast, and in New England, anything can happen weather-wise. Immediately, I decided I had to land.

Pushing the steering arm to full deflection, I lined up with the runway. At the time, It looked very inviting. There was plenty of room, and it was nice and flat. Heading into the wind, according to the wind sock, I leveled off at twenty feet and let the ParaPlane sink slowly onto the runway.

My glide slope was a bit steeper than I had anticipated, and I hit the runway pretty hard. This would not have been a problem ordinarily, but my arm was stiff as a board from tension, and when I hit the ground, my upper body which wasn't supported by the short boat cushion, leaned back from the impact, and caused me to push the throttle full forward. With the chute now falling, the ParaPlane lurched forward and pulled a wheelie.

Realizing what I had done, I pulled the throttle arm all the way back, shutting off the engines. The ParaPlane hung precariously, nose in the air, balancing on the two rear wheels. I thought for sure it was going to fall over backwards onto the props. I leaned my weight as far forward as the seat belt would allow, and finally, the nose came crashing down onto the runway, spinning the cart sideways as it did.

Everyone came running over as I removed my seat belt and packed the now wet chute. I was glad that my feet were on the ground. My father, Pip and Mike helped me to break the ParaPlane down as quickly as possible, and load it in the truck before it got any wetter than it was already. I had a funny feeling that the pilots at the airport didn't think too much of my performance, and I tended to agree with them.

Mike said he thought for sure I was going to flip over backwards on landing. Pip said he thought for sure I was going to hit the trees. My father said he thought I actually hit the parked plane on takeoff. He said I couldn't have missed it by more than an inch.

You might say that they were somewhat less than impressed with my abilities. It was obvious to all, including myself, that I had a lot to learn.

Fact is though, I learned a lot from my nearly disastrous second flight. I learned that the ParaPlane is a very forgiving aircraft. With all the lamebrained errors I made, I came out of it without a scratch. So did the ParaPlane. I could find no damage on it at all. Also, I learned that the wind had shifted just before I took off, and I neglected to check it. That was the reason for my erratic takeoff; the wind was actually behind me when I took off.

I should have checked the wind direction just before takeoff. I should have remained vigilant instead of becoming euphoric. I should have added a little throttle when I made my turns to stay level. I should have aborted my takeoff, when it first didn't seem right. I should have used a higher seat cushion for the proper upper back support. I should have used the grass instead of the runway for better control. I should not have taken off on the taxiway so close to the obstacles on the ground. I should have used every bit of space available for takeoff, in case of emergency. I should have used more common sense, and finally, I should not have been flying on a cloudy day with a rain storm predicted, and potential thunder and lightning. No question about it. I screwed up.

Flight number two had a stronger impact on me than I realized at the time. I became super cautious about weather conditions. Every time there was a cloud in the sky I wouldn't go. If the wind was blowing even a little bit, I would not fly. As anxious as I was to try it again, my overcautiousness would not let me go.

All through the months of June, July, August, September, and half of October, 1984, I did not fly the ParaPlane once. The best of summer had passed me by.

Finally, on a Thursday, the eighteenth day of October, under a crystal clear sky, with absolutely no wind to speak of, I set out for the airport.   I was shaking like a leaf.

It had been four and a half months since my last flight and most of my friends thought I had lost my nerve. They were pretty much on target with their assumption. I knew that I wouldn't get a better day than this, so if I didn't fly this time, I probably never would.

Pip and I set the ParaPlane up on the grass this time. After an extensive pre-flight, I started the engines, and buckled myself into the seat. My heart was pounding. Pip and Danny were holding the chute, waiting for my signal. All the problems from the last time were corrected. I had plenty of room on the grass strip. The weather was perfect. The wind was steady and very light, and I kept checking it constantly. Why then, was I so nervous? Once more, as with my first flight, I didn't think I could go through with it.

During the warm up period, I psyched myself up as best as I could, then flashed a thumbs up sign to my chute holders. Half throttle, and the chute came right up and opened fully. Everything looked perfect, so I went to full throttle and the cart climbed gently into the air.

What a fantastic flight it was! Absolutely nothing went wrong. I flew around for about twenty minutes, then made an easy soft landing on the grass, right next to where I took off. I was ecstatic! Now that I did it and it went so well, I was sorry I had waited so long. I was looking forward to getting a flight in on Saturday.

Between Thursday night and Saturday, I reveled in my new found confidence. On Saturday morning, I decided to take the ParaPlane out in my back yard, and give it a thorough pre-flight before flying in the afternoon. All the normal checks went well, and I decided to check out a few things that weren't part of the agenda. To my amazement, when I checked on the integrity of the outer propellor and its connection to the shaft, I found it loose! Something was definitely wrong. After removing the prop, I found that the shaft had cracked along the keyway. There would be no flying for me until this was corrected.

When I called the company, they asked me if I had ever rolled the cart over or damaged the props in any way. I told them I only had three flights and probably less than an hours flight time, with no damage to the props. They told me that it was highly unusual for that to happen under the circumstances.

Nevertheless, they told me it could be repaired free of charge, so I arranged to bring the power system to them personally for service. I wanted to see what kind of operation they were running, anyway.

New Jersey is their base of operation, which is about three hundred miles from my place. It was a very worthwhile trip on my part. I got to observe their research and design facility which is located in a hangar at a small airport. There, I met with their chief mechanical design engineer, a tall, thin, amiable man, whose name is Dan Thompson.

Dan was very concerned about the broken shaft problem, and went to work personally to repair it. He told me that he had never seen such a problem before on a unit with so little time on it, and with no prior damage. I assured him that I had done nothing to initiate this problem, and I sensed that he believed me. As he worked to change the broken shaft, I was allowed to watch, from a short distance away.

His mechanical expertise truly impressed me, and being a mechanical perfectionist of sorts myself, I marveled at his abilities. Within a short time, he had replaced the shaft, and tested the power system on one of their air frames. It ran like a clock with no sign that it ever had a problem in the first place.

Dan assured me that the cracked shaft would be X-rayed and examined to determine the cause of the break, and to negate any other potential failures. I thanked him for his efforts, loaded the power system in my trunk, and headed for home before the day was over.

As I drove back home, I felt reassured that the ParaPlane was a sturdy aircraft, well constructed by people who really knew what they were doing, and really cared about safety. Now, more than ever, I was looking forward to my fourth flight.

Over a month went by, though, and I still hadn't gone for my fourth flight. Every time I wanted to do it, some little thing or other would stop me.

Many times I would go to the airport and set everything up to fly, then decide it was too windy or too cloudy. Finally, on the twenty fifth of November, a Sunday, conditions looked optimum. I contacted Mike, and he, my father, and I arrived at the gate to the Fall River Airport at about eight in the morning.

For my previous three flights the temperature was in the sixty degree range. On this day it was only about thirty seven degrees Fahrenheit, but the visibility was excellent. Dressed up in much warmer clothes than necessary, I set everything up and pointed the cart into the light west wind.

My father, who hadn't seen a flight since the fiasco on the second one, was looking more than a little concerned. I really couldn't blame him, I had not shown him anything in the way of flying that could put him at ease.

One of my goals on this flight was to take some aerial photos, so I brought along a little instamatic camera. It fit nicely into one of the zipper equipped pockets on my parachute pants.

All the pre-flight checks went well, including the ones that I added. I briefed the ground crew, put in my ear plugs, donned my helmet, and started the engines. As I sat strapped into the cart, waiting for the engine warm up period, my heart was pounding.

This time though, I knew I was going to be able to do it. I signaled the ground crew that I was ready, and added some throttle. The cart started rolling and the chute began its rise overhead. However, the leading edge of the chute was folded under, so I pushed both steering arms full forward and released them, as previously instructed, to open the front of the chute and allow it to fully inflate. It worked like a charm, but I was running out of runway area.

Perhaps I should have aborted the takeoff, but my adrenaline rush had kicked in and I went immediately to full throttle. This time, the ParaPlane cart was hauled into the air much faster than last time. It was as if it were hooked to a giant sky crane, lifting it towards the heavens. The cooler weather and denser air, allowed for a much better climb rate.

Flying around the airport area, I took photos, and marveled at the breathtaking views afforded me. I took the ParaPlane up to nine hundred feet this time, and I could see all the way to Boston! This was the kind of flying I had always dreamed about. Alone in the sky with unlimited visibility. It was scary, but it was an awful lot of fun. I felt a freedom I had never experienced before. A whole new world had opened up before me, and I didn't want to land.

It was easy taking photos in the ParaPlane, since once you set the throttle where you want it, you can let go of it, and you have both hands free to do whatever you want. Your feet are also free, but I found it unnerving dangling them. Also, I still could not look straight down. It was too unsettling; I knew that I would have to wait until I had more experience.

My fuel was getting low, so I lined up for a landing. It was necessary for me to cross the runway on my landing approach, and I wasn't too crazy about it. I triple checked for planes landing or taking off by doing a full three hundred and sixty degree turn before entering the area. My approach was flawless, and I landed softly, right next to my car!

This time, I sensed that my father and Mike were impressed. They had good reason to be, as I think I made it look routine. The flight was excellent overall, except for some turbulence over an industrial parking area. It felt a bit weird, and the cart bounced up and down a bit, but it didn't last long, and it added some real excitement to the flight.

Now that the flight was history, I had time to relax and plan my next sky venture. I had hoped to fly again before the real cold weather arrived, but it wasn't to be. In fact, I did not fly again until late in the month of May, nineteen eighty five. In all of nineteen eighty four, I only flew four times. I vowed that the new year would be different, I would fly as much as I possibly could, and try to improve my skills. I planned to set some kind of goal for each flight and try my best to achieve it.

During the winter months, I stored the ParaPlane underneath the fuel oil tank in the cellar. I didn't really think I could fly it in the winter. I used the time to build a trailer. With it, I could carry the ParaPlane in its almost ready to fly state. In this manner I could be ready to fly at a moments notice, perhaps even after work in the evening when it stays light until almost nine o'clock.

I was looking forward with great anticipation, to the advent of Spring.

CHAPTER 5

THE SKY'S THE LIMIT

The Spring season was already two months old, and I had not flown the ParaPlane at all, since late in November of last year. My time was well spent though, as I had completed the trailer and the ParaPlane was sitting on it, waiting for the day when I would get up enough nerve to fly it.

On Wednesday, May twenty second, the weather was calm, cloudless and warm, so I decided to attempt a flight after work. Mike and Pip accompanied me to the airport. We had about two hours of daylight left, with a slight wind out of the south. This would be flight number five, if I could get up enough nerve to pull it off. My legs were shaking and my mouth was dry as I proceeded to pre-flight the ParaPlane extensively.

Much to my surprise, both of the small two cycle engines fired right up after a six month layoff period. Aiming into the slight wind, I buckled in and waited for the engines to warm up. During this three minute period, I tried to calm myself down and go through the entire flight in my mind, hoping to give myself some much needed confidence. I was very nervous.

Behind me, my chute holders were standing by patiently. It was time to fly and I was stalling. After a few more minutes of mentally kicking myself, I turned and signaled I was ready. In reality, I was far from ready, but from past experience I knew the longer I waited, the harder it would be to do it. It was now or never.

Surprisingly, the takeoff went very well, and before I knew it, I was soaring over the field at an altitude of five hundred feet. The warm upper air was exceptionally smooth, making me feel more at ease. I flew for about ten minutes, then decided to land.

Setting my sights on the spot I took off from, I flew in and landed gently, within a few feet of the launching site. It was about as good a flight as you would expect from an experienced pilot. I was really overjoyed! Especially now that I was back on the ground. It felt terrific to have finally flown after so long a wait.

As I was packing the chute in its black bag, Mike suggested that since it was still early enough, I should get another flight in. I hadn't even considered another flight, but there was at least a half hour of daylight left, so there wasn't any reason not to try again. I was glad he suggested it.

This time, I was a lot less nervous. Having just flown, I was more at ease, and confident that I would do well. In no time at all, I was back in the air for my sixth flight. The aerial view at dusk was breathtaking. I watched as the sun went down over the river. Many times I had seen the sun set while sitting in a lawn chair in my back yard. Now it was as if I was sitting in a lawn chair at seven hundred feet, and watching the sunset from a perspective I could not even have imagined before. If I could have relaxed just a little bit more, I would have really enjoyed it.

Nevertheless, this was by far my most enjoyable flight, and after another good landing, all I could talk about was how much fun I had. It was a long time between flights, and I promised myself that I wouldn't ever wait that long again.

Earlier in the year, I vowed to set a new goal every time I flew, in order to become as proficient a pilot as possible, and to experience all that I could. Not only one, but two new things were accomplished on this date. First, I saw the sunset, and second, I flew twice on the same day, back to back.

Even though everything went well on the fifth and sixth flights, it was a full month until I flew again. Deep inside, I was still nervous. If it wasn't dead calm, I wouldn't fly.

On June twenty second, a Saturday morning, I got in two flights and I was still quite nervous. I was beginning to wonder when, if ever, I would feel comfortable enough to really enjoy a flight. Thoughts of selling the ParaPlane crossed my mind, although I don't think I ever really would have.

My ninth flight on July second, was kind of a turning point. This was no calm day. My sister Anne from Chicago, was visiting with me. We usually only get to see each other once a year, and I wanted her to see me fly before she left. It was a Tuesday morning and I was on vacation. Anne would be leaving in a few days, and I felt I had waited long enough already. The wind wasn't too bad early in the morning, so I called Pip and asked him to meet us at the airport.

When we arrived, the wind was blowing at a steady ten miles per hour out of the north. Normally, I would never have flown under these circumstances, but the wind, although strong, was not gusting and I knew it would be possible to fly.

Pip and I set up the ParaPlane and I wheeled it out into the middle of the grass area between the taxiway and runway. In the open, you could really feel the wind, and Pip recommended that I postpone the flight until a later date. I seriously considered his advice, but I decided that I would have to fly, if I wanted my sister to see a flight before she left for home. We briefed Anne on how to hold the chute, and when to let it go.

As soon as I dumped the chute from the bag, the wind caught it, inflated it, and started dragging the cart to the rear. Quickly, I ran to the front of the cart, and grabbed it to prevent it from tipping over backwards. At the same time, I asked Pip and Anne to pull the chute down, and hold it on the ground until I was ready to go.

If I intended to continue flying the ParaPlane, I knew that sooner or later I would absolutely have to deal with the wind. I made up my mind that my goal for this flight would be the wind factor.

With the engines now warmed up, I flashed a thumbs up sign to Pip and Anne, indicating that I was ready. When they let the chute go, it soared overhead immediately, and I had to add quite a bit of throttle to hold the cart from being dragged backwards. I looked at the chute in the mirror, and it was fully inflated and ready for flight, and I wasn't even moving yet! Since everything looked good, I pushed the throttle full forward, and after rolling a mere twenty feet or so, I lifted off the ground.

My climb rate was good, but I had very little forward speed. As I reached four hundred feet, the wind speed seemed to equal my flying speed, and I was just hovering. Also, there was a considerable amount of turbulence. The cart was swinging back and forth, and up and down. It was quite unsettling, but I kept my wits about me and even managed to take a few photos.

As I turned in the direction of the wind, the ParaPlane really picked up speed. I was doing sixty miles per hour, judging from the way the ground was flashing by below me. Not wanting to get too far out of range, I turned quickly and headed back toward the field. In order to return, I had to drop my altitude down to a hundred feet, to get under the strong upper level winds. The bumpy air was starting to get to me, so I lined up for the area where Pip and Anne were standing. My landing was pretty fair considering the wind, and I landed almost on the same spot where I took off from. Anne and Pip pulled the chute down, and I killed the engines.

The wind was still strong, and I had a bit of trouble stuffing the chute into the bag, but eventually I won out. The flight was a little hair raising, but a complete success, nevertheless. I handled the wind quite well, and what really amazed me is that I was less nervous than usual. My confidence was building, and I was learning to feel more at ease.

Three days later on Friday morning, I flew two more times. My brother-in-law Steve had never seen a flight, and I was more than willing to accommodate him. The takeoff went well, with a new confident feeling.

The wind on the ground was out of the west at about eight miles per hour, but at five hundred feet, it was much stronger, out of the south. When I reached five hundred feet, I felt a little air turbulence, and as I turned south, I looked down at the earth and I was going backwards! The wind out of the south at that altitude must have been about fifty miles per hour! The feeling of going backwards while heading forward was a strange one indeed. I wasted no time in dropping my altitude to escape this powerful blast of air. As the ParaPlane descended, I felt the same weird bouncing sensation and then it was smooth flying again. Strangely, the experience didn't bother me very much, and I wasn't very nervous at all. I was starting to feel at home in the ParaPlane, with not quite as much anxiety. It was much calmer near the ground, with the wind out of the west, so I decided to take advantage of it and did some low to the ground flying.

Skimming along above the ground at say, three feet, is no easy task in a ParaPlane. I found it was necessary to constantly adjust the throttle and make subtle steering changes to keep flying straight and level. Adjustments had to be made slowly and precisely at the right time to prevent the cart from rocking and losing stability. It was very tricky and sometimes difficult to achieve, but after a while I got pretty good at it, and low flying became a lot of fun. Also, it allowed me to make a better landing.

On the second flight that day, I did a couple of touch and go landings, and additional low to the ground flying, which I was really starting to enjoy. Just before landing, I checked the wind sock, and was very glad I did. The wind had done a complete about face and was now out of the east at about five miles per hour. After aborting my first landing attempt, I turned around and landed into the new east wind.

In just these two flights, I achieved more aims than I would have expected in ten flights. And more importantly, I finally began to feel comfortable with flying the ParaPlane and being in the air. Nervousness was not completely absent though, and I didn't expect it ever would be. Sometimes, if you are too at ease, you could forget something very important. When it comes to flying, it could be hazardous to your health if you miss a pre-flight check, or forget some "simple" detail. Nervousness can be your friend in some cases. On July nineteenth, a Friday, I took a vacation day from work for my twelfth and most unconventional ParaPlane flight yet. At work, a lot of people were curious about my flying activity, so I decided to give them all a chance to see first hand what it was like, by flying over the facility.

There was a campground about a mile from the plant, with a very minimal field. It was only about two hundred feet by sixty five feet in area. After I requested permission to use it, and convinced the camp owners that I knew what I was doing, they reluctantly gave me the go ahead. Because of the small size of the field, I felt strongly that I would need at least a steady ten mile an hour wind, and it would have to be out of the south. Those were the predicted weather conditions for Friday, so I chanced a day off.

Pip, Danny, and Mike, accompanied me to the little field that morning. When we arrived the wind was gusting out of the south at a good twelve miles per hour. Pip and Danny held the chute down on the ground for me, while I started the engines, and Mike took some photos. The wind direction was perfect, but the field looked much smaller, now that I was sitting in the seat of the ParaPlane. I began to have second thoughts about flying from such a minimal field. In my head, I made some calculations, and decided that if I had a fully opened chute to start with, I could clear the tree line with ease. Pip and Danny let the chute go on my signal, and in seconds it was overhead and ready for flight. Although I was extremely nervous, I pushed the throttle to full, and released my foot from the front wheel. The cart took to the air within a few feet, and climbed almost straight up! At four hundred feet my forward motion was slowed to a mere crawl, and the air turbulence was tossing me all over the place.

It took about fifteen minutes to go a quarter mile, but I reached my destination and took some photos of the plant, despite the bumpy conditions. If I knew before I flew, exactly what it would be like, I believe I would never have flown that day.

Wind conditions seemed to be getting worse, so I turned around and headed back before my nervous stomach compelled me to. With the wind at my back, I returned to the field in less than a minute. As I spun around to land, the wind sock I had erected was now indicating a west wind at ground level. I...had a problem.

With the west wind, the only way I could land was across the short sixty five foot width of the field. To make matters worse, tall trees were on the east side of the field, and on the west side was a high chain link fence. I didn't know what to do. I looked around for alternative landing sites, but there didn't seem to be any in the general vicinity. If I flew with the wind for a while, I knew there would be some good sized areas to land in, but my ground crew wouldn't know where I was, since we had no radio contact.

Looking at the field from hundreds of feet in the air, gave it the appearance of a postage stamp. I needed a closer look, to get a better perspective. As I dropped in altitude, the cart rocked in the changing and gusting wind. My heart was pounding as I made a pass over the tips of the trees on the east side of the field, to attempt a landing. When I reached the edge of the tree line, I chopped the throttle back to idle, and the cart settled towards the ground. At about thirty feet, it became apparent that if I were to continue, I would hit the fence on the west side, so I pushed the throttle to full and aborted the landing.

By now, the wind was increasing in strength rapidly, but ironically, it was a blessing in disguise. On my second attempt to land, I was coming in much slower, because the ParaPlane is basically a constant speed vehicle, and the stronger winds slowed my forward speed. Again at the edge of the tree line, I brought the throttle to idle, but this time the ParaPlane dropped at a much steeper angle, giving me the precious extra feet I needed for a safe landing.

The impact was a little on the hard side, but I was never so happy to be on the ground, and the fence I expected to meet up with was twenty feet away! What an incredible learning experience flight number twelve turned out to be.

As a consequence of flight twelve, my next few flights were achieved with much less nervousness. In fact, by the end of the next month, I flew a total of fifteen times! All of these flights were out of the Fall River Airport, where there was plenty of open area to take off and land in any direction.

During these flights, I accomplished many of my goals. I practiced landings, with many touch and go's, did lots of low flying, tried short field takeoffs, flew with a video camera on my helmet, landed in slight crosswinds, and practiced low to the ground turns. My confidence was really building up, and now as I readied for a flight, what was once a feeling of dread, turned into an enjoyable sense of anticipation.

On Monday, August 19th, 1985, I received a form letter from ParaPlane Corporation, informing me that the first annual ParaPlane competition would be held on September 21st and 22nd, weather permitting. There were to be three different events consisting of a bomb drop, a precision altitude ribbon cut, and a hedge hop landing. Also, a banquet and some group flying were to be included. The letter read: "Fold your Para-Plane up, pack it in your trunk, and come on down!"

It seemed like a great way to meet some other people who also flew a ParaPlane, and since it was a month away, I figured that there would be plenty of time for me to practice for the events. I wanted to attend, mostly to meet others and exchange ideas; I really didn't think I was good enough to win anything. The only thing stopping me was that I didn't want to go by myself.

Fortunately, Mike was usually up for a weekend vacation, so I asked him if he would like to accompany me. Mike was undecided at first, but I convinced him we would have a good time, and eventually he agreed to go along. Now all I had to do was get in some practice flying.

On the previous weekend, the weather was great and I managed to get in a flight on Saturday and Sunday both. The

Saturday flight was unique in that I flew with a video camera attached to my helmet, and the recorder in a backpack strapped to my chest. It was awkward having all this equipment on me, so I didn't intend to stay in the air very long.

Tom Riley, a friend of mine who used to fly a fixed wing ultralight called a hummer, had suggested that I tape the cords and everything else down, to prevent any entanglement with the power system.

Although I was considerably nervous, the flight went well and I finally had an "in flight" video to show my friends and relatives. The only problem I had was getting all the duct tape off my body when the flight was over. Tom had plastered me good with the stuff, but it did the trick and kept anything from coming loose.

Sunday's flight was sheer enjoyment. The wind was calm and the visibility was excellent. When I reached eight hundred feet, I crossed the Taunton River and flew along the banks, taking in the gorgeous scenery. Crossing over the river at a narrow point upstream, I snaked my way back along the opposite side. The view was so clear that day, I swear I could see the mountains in New Hampshire. For the rest of the day, the scenes of the morning were vivid in my memory. Everything else that I did on that day, became pale by comparison.

With the competition a month away, I was anxious to accomplish some quality practice flights. On the following Friday, I took a half day vacation from work, to fly that afternoon. When I arrived at the airport though, the wind had picked up considerably and I was unable to fly. However, the following Saturday morning was a different story. The wind was out of the south at about nine miles per hour, and I decided to try my first cross country flight. Until now, I had always returned to the place I took off from. A cross country would take me to a place other than my launch site. About eight miles north of the Fall River Airport, there is a private grass airstrip called

Myricks. Earlier in the year, I spoke with the owner and he gave me permission to fly from there.

On this day, the wind was perfect to help push me there from Fall River. Pip volunteered to drive my car to the airstrip to pick me up. Shortly after my takeoff, as I was heading north toward the airstrip, I realized that I didn't know exactly where the field was located from the air. To avoid getting lost, I decided to follow the highway. Before long, I came to what I thought was the correct highway exit, but since I wasn't sure, I dropped my altitude low enough to read the exit sign. Sure enough, I had the correct exit, so I followed the road all the way to the grass field. It was probably not the greatest way to navigate, but at least I found the field. My landing was a little on the hard side because I wasn't familiar with the area, which made me a little more nervous than usual. Still, my first cross country was a resounding success.

The last week of August turned out to be very uncooperative weather-wise, as were the first two weeks of September. In fact, on the only weekend day that it didn't rain, I had already committed myself to doing a one hundred mile bicycle ride, and after finishing it, I was much too tired to attempt flying.

With the ParaPlane competition only a week away, I was desperate to get in at least one flight. After all, I hadn't flown in almost a month, how could I expect to fly in a competition? There was no doubt in my mind that on the first halfway decent day, I would absolutely have to fly at least once, to get the rust out and quell my nervousness.

Finally, on a Tuesday afternoon after work, with the wind blowing at a steady twelve miles per hour out of the south-southwest, I decided to try a flight. The competition was only three days away now, and weather predictions for the rest of the week were not good. It seemed this would be my last chance for a flight.

Pip and Danny met me at the airport, and as I was pre-flighting the ParaPlane, Pip suggested that it appeared to be too windy, and I should postpone the flight. Normally, I would have taken his advice, but this time, although conditions were border-line, I knew I was capable and decided to go ahead.

When I pulled the chute out of the bag, the wind caught the end, and it immediately started to inflate. While Pip and Danny struggled to hold it down, I ran to the front of the cart, and held it from being dragged backwards. Within seconds, the canopy was completely inflated so I had my ground crew hold the front of the cart while I started the engines. From the violent movement of the tops of the trees, I could tell the wind was going to be a major encumbrance.

It took a throttle setting of one half, just to hold the cart from moving backwards. My nerves were shot, and I was having second thoughts about flying. Nevertheless, I convinced myself that I knew what I was doing, and pushed the throttle to full. Before I had rolled ten feet, the ParaPlane swung up into the sky. As I climbed, the wind tossed the cart around like a puppet on a string. By the time I reached two hundred feet, I decided that I had experienced more than enough so I wasted no time turning around and setting up for a landing.

Ten minutes after takeoff, I was back on the ground and glad of it. The landing went well, but I needed some help getting the chute down in the wind. It was a very short flight and quite nerve wracking, but it sure did get the cobwebs out.

On Wednesday and Thursday, the weather proved to be unfavorable for para-flying. On Friday, Mike and I worked in the morning, and planned to take the rest of the day off to drive to New Jersey on the night before the competition. Before we left, I reflected back on my year and a half of exciting flight experience in the ParaPlane. I now had a total of twenty-seven flights and twenty three of them were in the last four months.

My fear of heights was becoming a memory. My confidence was building with every flight. Still, I really didn't think I had any chance of winning in a flight competition. How could I expect to compete against experienced pilots, with such little experience myself? After all, just a few short months ago, I had never flown anything in my life. I couldn't even climb a ladder without trembling. How in heavens name would I be able to do well in a contest?

Thinking about it was making me a nervous wreck, so I decided that if I wanted to enjoy myself, I would go just for the fun of it, to meet new people, exchange ideas and techniques, etc. There wasn't any sense in feeling uptight. I made up my mind to just do the best I could, and see what happens.

Mike and I left work at noon, and headed for New Jersey. The ParaPlane was folded and packed into the rear of my new small pickup truck. Since it was such a long drive, I didn't think it would be wise to use my trailer. During the trip my thoughts were wandering. Deep down inside, I really wanted to win something, and I had an ulterior motive.

For the past year, I had become heavily enamored with a local singer/songwriter and guitarist, named Barb Schloff. Her delightful and unique singing style combined with the sweetest voice I had ever heard, was mesmerizing. I couldn't stop listening to her, and I caught every one of her gigs. My greatest fantasy, other than flying, was to be a part of her life. After numerous vain attempts to win her affections, I finally resolved to be, as she put it, "just friends".

Still, as I motored along the coastal highways, I could not help but think of her. I thought perhaps if I could win something, it just might impress her enough to reconsider dating me. I suppose it was a foolish notion, but since I didn't have her anyway, I figured I had nothing to lose. At the very least, she was an inspiration for me to try harder.

Most aviation buffs, it is said, are incurable romantics. Who am I to argue? Oh...by the way...Remember those sleepless nights?

CHAPTER 6

THE COMPETITION

Sparkling rays of dawn were peeking through the folds in the motel curtains and dancing on my eyelids, as the alarm clock echoed in the new day. On the night before the competition, I fought off my anxiety attacks in hopes of sleeping well. I managed to get about six hours of sleep, but it was probably due to a couple of bottles of Guinness stout. When all else fails, I find Guinness stout usually does the trick.

That old feeling of nervous anticipation was returning, but unlike the evening, I now welcomed it as a means of waking up. As soon as Mike and I were ready to go, we left the motel and stopped off at a local diner for breakfast. Surprisingly, I began to feel at ease. I was looking forward to meeting some other ParaPlane owners and exchanging ideas. Since I didn't feel capable of finishing well in the competition, I finally decided to just fly for the fun of it and have a good time. After all, it was supposed to be a fun event, so I resolved to enjoy it. About a half hour after breakfast, we arrived at the Burlington County Airport.

The weather was gorgeous, but a touch on the windy side for so early in the morning. As we drove into the field, we could see numerous ParaPlanes in front of a huge white hangar building. I thought we were going to be too early, but it looked like we were the last ones to arrive. A rush of excitement came over me, and I hastily parked the truck near the side of the hangar.

Rounding the corner of the building, I was pleased to see such a good turnout. There must have been twenty five Para-Planes in front of the hangar. People were busy checking over their aircraft and adding fuel. I decided to go inside the hangar to see what was on the agenda. Talking to a group of people, was the inventor of the ParaPlane, Steve Snyder.

About a year ago at an air show I met Steve, but when I introduced myself this time, he didn't seem to remember me. He was busy fielding questions from a small group, and before I could get a word in edgewise, he called the whole group together for a pre-flight briefing.

Steve explained the scenario planned for the day's events. Each of us were to fly the three events in sequence. There was to be only one ParaPlane at a time in the sky. The bomb drop, which consisted of small bags of flour tied onto the air frame, would be the first event, followed by the precision altitude ribbon cut, then the hedge hop landing accuracy, or spot landing event. To give us a basic idea of how to approach each event, Steve said he would fly them all first. To assure safety, no Para-Plane would be allowed to fly without first being inspected by

Dan Thompson, ParaPlane's mechanical engineering whiz. After all the competitors finished the events, and if there was still time in the late afternoon, they had planned a cross country flight for the entire group.

Having completed the briefing, Steve announced that the order in which we flew would be determined by picking numbers out of a hat. There were twenty two people in attendance, and I picked number four. Since I had such a low number, I figured that I would get my flying in early, and just sit back and watch the other competitors do their thing, but ironically, it didn't turn out that way.

Now that we had our places picked, the next order of business was to line up all the ParaPlanes, tie them together with short ropes and hook them up to a pickup truck. The truck would then tow the so called "Para-train" across the street to a huge open grass field where the competition was to be held.

My ParaPlane was still in my truck in the folded state. Everyone else, it seemed, had brought their ParaPlane in on a trailer. They were all ready to go. I still had to assemble mine. Without wasting any more time, I set about the task of unloading and unfolding my ParaPlane.

As I frantically worked to restore my aircraft to a flyable state, a very professional looking man kept on taking pictures of my work in different stages. When I asked him why he chose to photograph me over the rest of them, he told me that I was the only one who had brought his ParaPlane to the event in the folded state. He said this was the way it was designed to be transported, so he wanted to have a record of it.

Within minutes, my ParaPlane was together and Dan was inspecting it. Meanwhile, Steve had called everyone, starting with number one, to line up in the proper sequence for their tow across the street. When he called the numbers, I didn't hear him because I was busy setting up. By the time I got through and approached him, he didn't want to rearrange things, so he assigned me the last spot.

During the fifteen minutes it took me to unfold the Para-Plane, I went from fourth in line to dead last. I was starting to regret leaving my trailer at home, but maybe it was a blessing in disguise. Since I now had twenty one competitors scheduled to fly ahead of me, the only logical thing to do was sit back and watch them do their thing.

Mike and I settled down in the grass field along with the other spectators, and watched as Steve Snyder demonstrated in seemingly easy fashion, how to fly the three events properly. He really made it look like child's play. If any of the competitors were half as good, I figured that there wasn't much chance of me winning anything.

Soon the competition was underway, and it was rather enjoyable to relax and just watch the others fly. As each person went through their routine, it became apparent that the course was not as easy to fly as Steve made it seem. Before long, I was able to analyze what each person was doing wrong, and I worked out a possible solution for each little mistake in judgment that they made.

During the bomb drop, most pilots didn't take into consideration the strength of the wind. They had to drop their small plastic bag of flour (bomb) from an altitude of at least one hundred feet. The dropping altitude was decided by an official on the ground, and if he didn't think you were sufficiently high enough, he would wave you higher. Since the bag weighed very little, the fairly strong winds of about ten knots, would usually push it far away from the target area. Some pilots, who probably watched the others as I did, dropped the bag quite a distance after passing the target, thereby allowing the wind to carry the bag onto the target zone. After about ten competitors had flown, many were hitting the target with accuracy and regularity. It looked simple enough to me.

In the precision altitude ribbon cutting event, it seemed that everyone was having a lot of trouble. Two orange ribbons, separated by about two feet, were stretched between two poles about ten feet high and fifteen feet apart. The object was to fly into the top ribbon, cutting it with the landing gear only, without cutting the bottom ribbon. You would receive 300 points if you cut the top ribbon with the front landing gear, and 150 points if you cut it with either of the rear wheels. Cut it with anything else, or break the lower ribbon too, and you get no points at all. Also, if after you cut the ribbon, you came in contact with the ground, you receive no points. A pilot had to remain airborne in order to qualify successfully. As I watched, most pilots either missed the thin ribbons completely, or blasted through both ribbons. Very few were able to fly through with accuracy.

Soon it became apparent to me what the problem was. Pilots were dropping down to the attack altitude zone too late to allow the ParaPlane to stabilize. When they added throttle to level off, they were too close to the intended target for the ParaPlane to attain stability. I knew from my low flying experience how difficult it can be to fly straight and level if you have to make major throttle or steering corrections.

The solution, it seemed to me, was to get down to attack altitude long before you're anywhere near the target. This would allow you an abundance of time to stabilize the craft, get it to fly straight and true, so you would have a better chance of hitting the ribbon dead on. Again, I felt the problem was solved.

The hedge hop landing accuracy event presented a whole new set of problems. Here, the intent was to fly over the ribbons without hitting them, and then land in a marked target zone that was immediately on the other side, setting the front wheel down as close to the center as possible. In order to hit the target, it was necessary to barely miss hitting the ribbon.

This was more of a comedy act than an event. Pilots were either hitting the ribbon or missing the target completely. Some pilots, especially the heavier ones, came in at such extreme angles that they broke the front wheel off on impact with the ground. Others flipped their carts over backwards! Still others, with lengths of florescent ribbon trailing from their landing gear, did not even bother to land. It was hilarious! Best of all, no one got hurt. One fellow, after taking off again for another attempt at a spot landing, turned with the wind at too low an altitude and crashed into a plowed field. He kicked up a huge cloud of dust on impact, and was upside down in the cart when we reached him, but he was unhurt! All of the accidents I saw were due to pilot errors, and not the fault of the ParaPlane. This really impressed me. I couldn't think of a single thing a person could do wrong, other than deliberately flying into a power line, that would cause any serious injury. My confidence in myself and in the craft, was at an all time high.

Still, this didn't make it any easier to figure out how to fly this event successfully. Not very many pilots were able to spot land accurately. It was very difficult to come up with a satisfactory solution to this problem. Finally, I decided to use the same technique for this event that I came up with for the last one. I would fly in from far away, this time aiming for the center of the target and after passing over the top ribbon, chop the throttle back to idle at the precise instant that the drop angle would put me on center. It seemed logical, but I didn't know if it would work until I tried it. I was getting extremely anxious to fly.

By mid afternoon, about sixteen competitors had completed their events. I still had about five people ahead of me. The wait was beneficial in that it gave me a chance to analyze the events and come up with a strategy of my own, but I was getting very restless. The next competitor in line was having trouble starting his ParaPlane, so I asked if I could take his place, as long as no one else objected. Since I was ready to go, and no one protested, they decided to let me fly next. There was no reason for me to think that I would do any worse than the rest of them, but still, I was a bit nervous while getting ready to fly.

Five clear plastic bags of flour were ty-wrapped onto the air frame of my ParaPlane. I was assigned a little ring for my finger that had a small knife blade attached to it. The blade was to be slipped under the ty-wrap and pulled when I was ready to drop a "bomb". The wind was still blowing at about nine knots as I started my takeoff run.

Within seconds, I was in the air and climbing up to bomb drop altitude. My pulse was racing, not so much from nervousness, but more from sheer excitement! It was very exhilarating having a chance to compete in an event that most assuredly was the first of its kind. I felt really in control and on top of the world.

At one hundred feet, I leveled off and headed for the bomb drop target. As I approached the target, the official person on the ground waved me higher. My altimeter read 120 feet, but it was his show, so I climbed higher and went around for another pass. This time the altimeter read 150 feet, but still he waved me higher. Another go-round, and I was starting to think I forgot to set my altimeter at ground level. On this pass, it read 200 feet, but this time he gave the "OK" signal. Without thinking, I let one of the bombs go directly over the target. The wind took it so far away from the target, I couldn't even tell where it landed! Fortunately, the first try on each event was only for practice and not for points.

Without knowing where the bag landed, I had no way of calculating the necessary adjustment. The next try proved to be a waste also. I flew quite a bit past the target, but still I missed it. This time though, I saw where it landed. The rest of my drops landed on the target, however, none of them were anywhere near the center. I knew from watching the others, that a lot of them had better scores than me, so I chalked it up to experience, and headed for the ribbon cutting area. Even though I knew I did terrible in the bomb drop, it didn't bother me much because it was a heck of a lot of fun!

Now, this was the moment I had been waiting for. Whether I did well or not was no longer a question. I figured my score in the previous event would negate any chance of my winning. The pressure was off now, so I could concentrate on doing the best I knew how, and not worry about the outcome.

Down at the far end of the huge field, I turned around and pulled the throttle back to idle. My basic intent was to allow for as much distance between me and the ribbons as possible. Within a few feet of the ground, I leveled off and headed into the wind towards the target. My strategy was working perfectly. After leveling off and stabilizing the cart, I still had a few hundred feet to go. I sat as motionless as I could, making only very slight steering corrections and slow easy throttle adjustments. Even though it was windy, I approached the ribbons almost rock steady and at the closest I could come to proper altitude. At the last second, with only a few feet to go, I made some final corrections, and a sudden gust of wind blew me into the pole holding the ribbon. This was only my practice run, and although I hit the pole, I knew my altitude was right on target. All that remained now was to repeat what I knew I could do, and hope for a steady wind.

Every approach after the first went exactly as I had planned it, but although I knew I hit the ribbon with either the front or rear landing gear, I couldn't tell if I had hit the bottom ribbon or not. After I passed through the target, I couldn't see behind me. By the time I gained some altitude and turned around for another pass, they had restrung the ribbon. Still, I knew I did a lot better on this event than in the last one.

Now it was time for the final event, the spot landing. As in the ribbon cutting, I set up my approach from the far end of the field. This time though, I had to fly in a few feet higher to clear the top ribbon. On my first attempt, just as I passed over the top ribbon, I chopped the throttle all the way back to the idle position. The center of the target was directly in front of me. My drop angle seemed perfect. I held my breath and a few seconds later, my front wheel touched down right in the middle of the nine inch red spot in the center of the target! I was elated!

While the chute was still overhead, I pushed the throttle full forward and lifted into the air again. Grinning from ear to ear, I swung around for another pass. Then it dawned on me. I had made a perfect spot landing, but it didn't count for points. It was only a practice run. Now I had to try to repeat it four more times.

One of my spot landings during the New Jersey Competition.

My confidence was at a high point. All I had to do was mimic the first run and I should have no trouble hitting at least close to the center. Four more times I flew, with every bit of precision I could muster, but none of the runs were as accurate as the first. Still, every landing was within three feet of the center, with at least two of them touching the center spot!

Satisfied with my performance, I brought the ParaPlane down close to where I took off from. It was a good feeling knowing I had at least done my best. After packing the chute away, I saw my friend Mike coming toward me. I asked him what he thought of my performance. He said that he didn't think I had done that bad, but he really didn't see all of the others fly, so he couldn't tell exactly how I had performed overall. However, he told me that Steve Snyder seemed to be impressed with my flying.

We spent the next hour watching the remainder of the competition. When it was over, we walked over to the end of the field near the road, where a group of pilots were congregating. Some were discussing the upcoming cross country flight. Others were talking about a head to head competition in spot landing, which was to take place on the following day between Steve Snyder and a man named "Carr".

Assuming that there must have been another person in the group with my last name, I asked them who Carr was. The overwhelming response was, "you are!"

"Me?...Why me?" I asked.

"You have the most points overall," they said. "So far, you are the winner of the competition."

I stood there motionless, not knowing whether or not to believe them. It took a few more questions to finally convince me that the group was telling me the truth. I couldn't believe it. I was stunned. It seemed that everyone there knew about it but me. Never in my wildest dreams did I really think I had a chance to win anything, but I did it! I had to find out more. Talking to some of the officials, I was told that I had amassed enough points to take the overall Grand Champion Award! At least up to this point. They informed me that tomorrow, four more people were to compete that couldn't make it on Saturday, so it was still possible I could be beaten. They couldn't tell me at this time, which of the categories I had done better in, I would have to wait until the competition was over.

After the initial shock of having done so well wore off, I began to look forward to the rest of the days activities. With a few hours of daylight left, there was still time for the planned cross country flight. All twenty two entrants decided to join in. The sight of all those multi-colored chutes billowing out in the warm afternoon sun was something to behold. One by one, each of us took off and flew around in a big circle, waiting for everyone to become airborne. We were instructed to follow Steve Snyder, who was easy to spot with his bright yellow canopy.

Steve headed out over the farms and fields with the rest of us in pursuit. At seven hundred feet, I leveled off. For the first time in my life, I was able to relax in the ParaPlane, safe in the knowledge that I really knew what I was doing. The only thing that was somewhat unsettling was flying with all the other Para-Planes around me. Everywhere I looked, there were canopies in the sky, and they all seemed to be flying a little bit faster than I was. They were below me, above me, and on both sides. And they were passing me, ever so slowly.

Since I only weigh 130 pounds, I fly about a half mile an hour slower than the advertised 26 mph speed of the ParaPlane. To compensate for this, I decided to cut some corners. Whenever Steve turned in any direction, instead of following like everyone else, I turned at the same time, giving me a more direct route. By doing this, I was able to keep up with the whole group.

At one point in the flight, over a particularly scenic winding river, Steve dropped down in altitude and began flying along the river bank. Everyone else maintained altitude and just sort of flew around in a big circle over him. He looked like he was having fun, and I saw no reason not to join him, so I did. Within minutes, I was flying behind him, not too close, just below the tree tops. It was an incredible experience! The grandeur of nature at this altitude was absolutely overwhelming. The river was about twenty to sixty feet wide, with high trees on its banks. The shoreline was sandy with ample room for an emergency landing. In spots, the entire surface of the river was covered with dark green lily pads. I marveled at being able to see some of nature's wonders from such a unique vantage point.

Because of the slow flying speed design of the ParaPlane, we had ample time to take in the sights and make any necessary course corrections. Soon, however, the river began to narrow and Steve took his ParaPlane back up to cruising altitude, with me in hot pursuit. Joining the others, we headed back out over the scenic countryside. The sun was setting on the horizon, offering a red streaked view through wispy clouds. As we made our way back to the field, I looked at my watch and realized we had been in the air for over an hour. With only an eighth of a tank of fuel left, and the field in view, I decided to cut the trip short and head back. Some of the other pilots did the same. They were probably also low on fuel. Within ten minutes of my landing, which went very well, all the others had returned, except for one.

They sent a crew out to look for the missing pilot in the vicinity of where he was last seen. When they returned a short time later, we heard the full story. It seems the pilot became euphoric, and didn't bother to check his fuel supply. He ran out of gas and landed in a corn field next to the road. He was in great shape, but probably a little embarrassed.

All in all, the cross country was a resounding success. After stashing our ParaPlanes in the hangar, everyone left to get ready for the planned spaghetti banquet.

Mike and I were leaving for the motel, when we met a young man named John Ferguson, whom we had befriended earlier. He had taken his first flight earlier in the day, and had only his ten speed bike for transportation. He was afraid he wouldn't make it home in time to attend the banquet. We offered him a ride and he readily accepted. Shortly thereafter, the three of us arrived at the restaurant and went inside.

The meal was very good, and we spent a lot of time socializing and getting to know one another. Steve Snyder announced that at this time, it appeared that I was the overall winner of the event, with over eleven hundred points. I knew there were more people coming tomorrow, but for now, it was nice to bask in the spotlight. People were asking me all sorts of questions about flying. They wanted to know who had trained me, and how I got to be so good.

I told them that I more or less trained myself, and that I really didn't think I was very good until today. Before the competition, I never had anyone to compare myself against. Doing as well as I did took me by surprise.

Later that evening, Steve announced that he had planned a morning "breakfast flight," and anyone who wanted to go along must be at the field by seven thirty sharp. This really intrigued me. It sounded like a lot of fun. Since it was getting late, I asked Mike if he wanted to leave now, so we could get up early in the morning. Mike loves to eat, and it seemed like he was enjoying this part of the trip the most. I hated to tear him away, but he agreed to leave, so we said goodnight to everyone, and hit the road. Some of the group were just starting to get into a party mood, so only a few people left around the time that we did.

That night I slept well. Numerous thoughts of the days activities washed through my mind, but somehow I managed to get to sleep fairly quick. A bottle of Guinness stout, and a new feeling of security helped me to doze off.

Seven hours later, the alarm clock rang, giving us one hour to get to the field by seven o'clock. When I looked out the window into the dull gray of early morning, I couldn't even see my truck. The fog was as thick as pea soup. Hoping that the fog would lift, Mike and I got ready anyway, and headed for the flying field. On the way, I noticed that the fog was only in patches and about fifty feet thick. It was basically a ground fog. The sky above was clear.

When we arrived at the field, some pilots were already pushing their ParaPlanes across the roadway. I grabbed my helmet and joined them. This time around, my unfolded aircraft was flight ready. The morning air was still nippy, so I decided to wear the winter jacket that I brought along. I also took my camera with me.

By the time we had set up to fly, it was after seven o'clock and the fog was lifting. Looking over the group, I counted fourteen of us. The rest of the group probably stayed too long at the restaurant, and couldn't get up in time. I had a feeling they were about to miss out on the best part of the trip.

One at a time, we took off into the misty ground fog, and flew around above it until all were airborne. The air was unbelievably calm. It was like flying on rails. By shifting my weight slightly in the seat, I could make tiny course corrections without pushing the steering arms. It was great! I sat back, crossed my legs and enjoyed the flight.

At the beginning of the flight, I took the lead, knowing that I fly a bit slower than the rest. This proved to be advantageous, in that I was able to stay near the front of the pack.

About forty minutes into the flight, I noticed our leader, Steve, dropping in altitude. He never told us exactly where we were going, but it appeared to be a diner by the side of an intersecting roadway. Across the road from the diner was a baseball field. Steve dropped down over a corn field and flew in low onto the baseball field. It appeared to me that he made a spot landing right on home plate! What a piece of flying! Dropping down over the corn field, I made my approach in a similar style. I landed right next to Steve, at the top of the field.

ParaPlanes were dropping out of the sky all over the field. It was an awesome sight. Many cars were stopping on the side of the road to witness a never before seen event. A motorcycle gang pulled over to watch. There was a carnival like atmosphere. As I packed my chute away in its bag, one of the motorcycle riders came over. This is how the dialogue went:

"What the hell is that thing, anyway?"

It's a ParaPlane, a powered parachute."

"How much does it cost?"

"Prices vary; I got mine for about four grand."

"Wow! That's cheaper than my motorcycle!"

"I don't doubt it for a minute."

"And it looks like a lot more fun!"

"Most fun you can have with your pants on!"

The biker walked away muttering something about looking into purchasing one. After he left, we were deluged with questions by a number of curious onlookers. It was fun extolling the virtues of flying to people. Steve interrupted, saying it was time for breakfast, so we all walked across the street to the diner. I felt like a celebrity.

As we crossed the roadway, I looked back and noticed a number of spectators were checking out the fourteen Para-Planes that we left behind on the ball field. Worried that something might happen to them if we left them unattended, I asked Steve if we shouldn't maybe leave someone behind to keep an eye on them. He laughed and said, "Don't worry about it. Nobody will touch them. People are generally bewildered by them. They will look out of curiosity, but they won't lay a hand on them." Perhaps he was right, but I would have felt better if someone had stayed behind.

Many of the pilots had told their families where we were going for breakfast, so quite a number of them showed up in their cars and trucks. Had I realized this beforehand, I would have told Mike to meet us. I felt bad that he had to wait back at the airfield. At least there was a restaurant where he could eat breakfast.

When we entered the diner, I was amazed at the size of the interior. The place looked tiny from the outside, but inside it was huge. There were tables set up for us. Steve had prearranged the whole thing. We proceeded to take our seats, and I was fortunate enough to have gotten a seat across from Steve.

Before long, we had all placed our orders and began to get better acquainted with one another. The man sitting next to me introduced himself as Gene Flores. He had only a few flights under his belt, and confessed that he was still quite nervous. He also revealed a fear of heights. I marveled at the strange parallel he was drawing between the two of us, but the real shocker was when he told me where he was from.

"I'm from Marion, Massachusetts," he said.

"No kidding! I'm from Fall River!"

"I don't believe it! We're almost neighbors!"

It was a strange analogy. Of all the people there, he lived the closest to me, and just happened to be sitting right next to me. We talked at length about our experiences with flying and fear, and I assured him that soon he would feel more at ease in the sky. He seemed skeptical, and I really related to that.

Everyone was in a festive mood for such an early hour. The room was buzzing from the sound of electric conversations. There were men and women, young and old, and all of us were celebrating the natural high brought on by our early morning flight.

Gene and I were both engrossed by a story that Steve related to us about how the ParaPlane evolved. We listened intently, as his tale unfolded while we ate our breakfast. This is how I remember it.

Along with his two partners, Dan and Ed, Steve worked feverishly to come up with a working prototype. One of the biggest events in ultralight aviation was coming up soon. There was very little time left before an event known as "Sun n'Fun" in Florida was to take place. Day and night they labored, taking only an occasional break for short periods of sleep. Finally, after weeks of steady toil, their working prototype was ready. But it had never been tested, and there was no time left for a maiden flight. It was four in the morning and they had to be in Florida that afternoon to catch the last day of the event. Although they were mentally tired and physically exhausted from their ordeal, they loaded the ParaPlane prototype on Steve's plane and left New Jersey before the light of day.

When they arrived in Florida, one of their worst fears was realized. It was windy. Very windy. It was also their last opportunity that year to introduce the ParaPlane. They knew if they were ever going to fly, it would have to be that afternoon. Because of the wind conditions, most of the fixed wing ultralights stayed grounded.

The wind would not relent, and time was running out, so Steve made the decision to go for it. They wheeled the ParaPlane out into the open, and laid out the chute. Instantly, the chute rose into the air, billowing out in the strong winds. As his associates held the cart, Steve started the engines and buckled himself in. The winds were blowing at about twenty five miles per hour. These were far less than ideal conditions for flying an ultralight.

As apprehensive as he was about the weather conditions, Steve felt confident he could take the ParaPlane up safely. He pushed the throttle forward. Crowds of people were standing by to witness for the first time the launching of a strange new ultralight aircraft, and what a show they got! To everyone's amazement, the ParaPlane took off straight up like a helicopter! The winds were evidently blowing at a speed equal to the fixed flying speed of the ParaPlane, thereby allowing a vertical takeoff.

Conventional ultralight pilots were astonished to witness such a capability in an ultralight. The demonstration was a resounding success. Steve floated around for a while, then landed the ParaPlane without incident. On a day when no self respecting ultralight pilot wanted to fly, the ParaPlane came through with "flying colors." People were instantly very curious, and Steve was already receiving orders for a craft that wasn't even in production yet.

By the time Steve finished telling us his story, Gene and I were polishing off the remainder of our breakfast. Most of the people in attendance finished eating at about the same time, so we paid our bills and headed outside. As I exited the diner, I took a deep breath of the clean fresh morning air. The sun was shining brightly, and the scattered ground fog was nowhere to be found. Upon crossing the roadway, I wondered if the flight back to the field might cause air sickness, since my stomach was more than a little full. In all of my previous flights, I made it a point to fly on an empty stomach. This time I would find out if it really mattered. At least I had company. I was not going to find out alone.

In the field, I checked for wind and could not detect even the slightest breeze. One of the officials had set up a flare in the center of the field. It indicated by its smoke that there was a light drift toward the top of the field, where we had landed. Everyone headed to the other end of the field to set up, but I had to wait.

The gas tank on my ParaPlane was less than half full. There was no way I could make it back on less than half a tank. Fortunately, the ground crews of some of the other participants had driven to the diner, and some of them brought along extra gasoline. When I offered to purchase some, they said, "no way."

Disgruntled at what I thought was their lack of compassion, I began to walk away, and they stopped me. They didn't want any money. They wanted to give me the fuel for free. I felt like a real jerk. Normally, I expect to pay for whatever I acquire.

After topping off my tank and announcing my appreciation for the gas, I headed to the other end of the field where most of the pilots were now ready to fly. With our wings flapping in the prop wash, we waited our turn as an official signaled us to go, one by one. When my turn came, I pushed the throttle full forward as soon as my chute was open to allow for the shortest possible takeoff run. Seconds later, I was in the air and circling the field, waiting for the rest of my fellow aviators to join the "squadron." As I looked out over the green and yellow cornfields from my perch on high, I thought, "What a great way to really see the countryside."

Another reason for my euphoria was the dead calm air. It felt like I was floating on a magic carpet. I couldn't remember when I had experienced a smoother flight than this. All thoughts of possibly becoming airsick were gone from my mind. It felt good to have a full stomach and not be concerned.

Soon we were all airborne and heading for the airfield. Maintaining an altitude of eight hundred feet, I scanned the beautiful farmlands and kept a sharp eye out for other Para-Planes that wandered too close to me. Occasionally, I noticed a ParaPlane flying very low over the farmhouses, perhaps to get a better view. The idea was tempting, but I was sure the people in the homes would take a dim view of a loud aircraft buzzing their domiciles at such an early hour. I decided to maintain my altitude and enjoy the view from a distance. My little "sky chair" was performing beautifully as we approached the airfield.

Circling the field, I waiting for most of the others to land, so I could enjoy the breathtaking views for as long as possible. My gas tank was below half full when I landed. Without the extra gas, I surely would have run out.

The last to land was Steve Snyder. He made his approach to the field with both engines off, and he landed with the wind instead of against it. His angle of approach was not too steep, even without power, due to his increased ground speed. The quiet landing was relatively soft, and the only consequence was that the chute came over his head and landed in front of him as he rolled to a stop. This proved to me that in an emergency situation, you can land safely and soften your touchdown by landing with the wind, if need be.

Four more competitors arrived that morning and by early afternoon, they had completed their events. Some pilots did quite well, since the wind conditions were much more favorable than on Saturday. At this point, I had no way of knowing if they had beaten my scores.

Now that the competition was over, Steve told us that he and his chief instructor, Nathan Taylor, would fly in a spot landing competition against me. It was quite obvious now, that I had the most points overall and although I was elated, I was apprehensive about competing against Steve and Nathan. After all, they had more experience flying a ParaPlane than anyone in the world.

At Steve's prompting, all the other pilots and crew members formed a pool, and bet money on the event. The premise was that half of the money would go to the winner, and the other half would be distributed to those who bet on him. Now I was really getting a case of the jitters. People were coming over and asking if they should bet on me. I told them to bet on whoever they liked, but to remember that I was basically a beginner and might have just gotten lucky flying in the competition. Nevertheless, I assured them that I would give it my best shot. Quite a number of them bet on me, including Mike, which only served to increase my nervousness.

It was decided by the powers that be, that I would fly first and Steve and Nathan would try to beat my score. The sky was getting darker with some ominous looking clouds approaching. It appeared to be just a passing squall line, and I wanted to fly before it came in, but they made me wait. No rain was associated with it, but as it passed by, the inevitable wind picked up considerably. At that point, Steve said it was time for me to fly. The wind wasn't very strong, but it was gusting and changing direction. Although I really didn't care for the conditions, I was anxious to fly, and took to the sky. Gathering up every bit of courage and self reliance, I made my first approach to the target. It was very difficult stabilizing the cart for an accurate landing due to the changing wind currents.

Upon clearing the ribbon, a gust blew the cart sideways and although I corrected for it, I was soon on the ground and ten feet from the center of the target. Frustrated with my poor performance, I jammed the throttle full forward, and soon I was lining up for my second attempt. This time the wind direction changed so dramatically, they had to reposition the poles that held the ribbons. The little cart was gyrating back and forth, at the command of the changing winds. My second attempt was not much better than the first, and the last three tries, although much more accurate, were not nearly as good as I would have liked.

My pride was hurt, but I did my best, and if the conditions remained the same, the pressure was off me and on them. Still, I would have preferred to have competed under better conditions.

As Nathan was preparing for takeoff, the fickle winds started to calm down. I could see my chances of winning fading away with the breeze. Nathan flew the course like the consummate professional that he is. Although there was still a bit of wind to contend with, he managed five spot landings that seemed a little more accurate than mine were, overall.

Soon after Nathan's flight, Steve took to the sky. The winds were now considerably less than when Nathan flew, and much less than when I flew. It was soon evident that Steve was going to come out of this on top. He was clearly the most accurate on all of his landings, and when they announced the scores, Steve had the most points. All three scores were fairly close and I was satisfied with the results even though I lost. It was really a lot of fun competing against the two people who probably know more about flying in a ParaPlane, than anyone else in the world.

Steve was given his share of the winnings and with that, he called all of us out into the open field. Everyone stood around him in a tight circle as he proceeded to commend the group for following the rules and making the event a success. Since he invented the ParaPlane and knew more about it than anyone, he told me not to feel bad that I didn't beat him. As he spoke, he held the wad of money in his hand and waved it around in the air.

"This money belongs to everyone!" he shouted, as he flung it into the air over our heads. It was raining greenbacks, and everyone scrambled and grabbed for a share of the loot. Mike managed to retrieve exactly what he had bet, and I ended up with exactly what I had bet...nothing.

Shortly thereafter, we assembled in the hangar building for the awards ceremony. To my surprise, I not only received the Grand Champion Award for the most points, I also took First Place in the ribbon cutting and First Place in the spot landing. When it came time to announce First Place in the bomb drop, Steve said, "guess who won this one?" and since I seemed to be the choice, everyone yelled, "John Carr!" I held my breath, but it wasn't me. It was actually a relief to me that someone else won, my knees were like jelly when I went up to receive my three plaques.

After all the awards were distributed, Steve asked me to say a few words with regards to how I had accomplished the win. Since I was so delirious, and unprepared, I blurted out something about precision throttle control and a little bit of luck. I was too overwhelmed by the whole affair to put together in words exactly how I did it. The whole scenario seemed more like a dream than reality. Cameras were flashing in my face and the whole crowd in front of me looked like a blur. After thanking everyone, I happily turned the floor over to Steve Snyder.

Steve stressed the point that there was a lot you could do in a ParaPlane with a little practice. He also thanked everyone again for making the first annual ParaPlane competition a resounding success.

The Competition Winners.

With the closing of the event, Mike and I said good-bye to some of the people we met, and packed the ParaPlane in the back of the pickup truck. Before leaving for home, I talked to Gene Flores again and we agreed to get together back home for some fun flying.

My friends, Marc and Donna deVillers, from New Jersey, had attended at my invitation to cheer me on. They joined Mike and I for a quick meal on the way back home at a fast food restaurant. Elation must have been written all over my face, judging from my friends comments about my grinning from ear to ear, while wolfing down a greasy cheeseburger.

During the trip back home, I thought about the fact that I had triumphed in the first and only factory sponsored ParaPlane competition. In effect, this achievement could allow me to bill myself as a World Champion! Why not? It was the world's first event...John Carr...World Champion ParaPlane Pilot! Wow! It sounded good to me. I couldn't wait to get home and tell all my friends. They'll never, never believe it, especially those who knew how much of a vegetable I was in the beginning. Most of all though, I couldn't wait to see the look on Barb's face, when I would tell her I am a World Champion. Although I wanted to impress her, I never dreamed that I would come back home with this much ammunition.

With my mind filled with thoughts of reactions from everyone I knew, the three hundred mile ride back home seemed to be incredibly short. I was at peace with the world.

CHAPTER 7

HEAD IN THE CLOUDS

Singing and smiling is not the way I normally face a Monday morning. On this morning however, I couldn't wait to get to work. It's amazing how feeling good about yourself can perk up your whole day. I awoke earlier, got ready earlier, arrived at work earlier, and I felt like I was sitting on top of the world.

At work, all through the day, I relished telling any of my co-workers who would listen, the whole story of how I won the championship. My three plaques were proudly displayed on the top of my desk for all to see. It was obviously very difficult to get any work done. People came over to congratulate me all morning, as word of my accomplishment spread throughout the department. It felt good to know that some of my friends were genuinely impressed. Others showed signs of disbelief, and some people who did not even know that I flew, were somewhat amazed and more than a little curious. Without a doubt, I was thoroughly enjoying my new status, but it was the evening that I was really looking forward to.

At a local area nightclub where my singer friend Barb doubled as a waitress, I had become a regular customer. Some of the people who frequented the club, and the waitresses and bartenders, knew I had gone down to New Jersey for the competition. On this Monday evening, Barb was going to be performing and I couldn't wait to tell her the news of my win.

When I got home from work, I packed my three award plaques and some photos into a case and headed for the club. Purposely, I arrived at the club early to give Barb a chance to hear my story before she went on. I'll never forget the look on her face when I walked over and told her that I won the ParaPlane Grand Championship. Her face lit up with a smile that could warm the coldest of hearts. With affection she said,

"John, that's great! That's terrific! Wow, I can't believe it!" It was one of the happiest moments of my life and I will always remember it fondly.

To say that I was enamored of her would be the understatement of the century. She made the entire night with her initial reaction, and even announced over the mike that I was the ParaPlane World Champion!

I would have done anything to win her over, but deep down inside, I knew that she and I would never be. She had made it perfectly clear in the past that she liked me only as a friend. Nevertheless, I wasn't going to let anything spoil my fantasy for the evening. After all, if I hadn't been thinking of impressing her, I doubt if I would have done as well competing. She didn't know it, but she was indirectly responsible for my winning performance. If only we could be more than friends. If only.

By the end of the night, I was feeling the glow of the warm reception I received, not to mention the glow from a number of Guinness stouts. With a work day ahead, I should have left the club earlier, but I enjoy her singing and guitar playing so much, I can never leave before she has completed her performance.

On my way home, thoughts of what I would do on my next flight ran through my mind. The ego building I had received all night fueled my thoughts. Only thirty two flights ago I had never flown a ParaPlane. Now I was a Champion. The next flight had to be special.

All week long, I tried to get a flight in after work, but the weather would not cooperate. Because I wanted this next flight to be something special, I wanted to be sure the weather would be as close to perfect as possible.

After work, in the evenings, I spent most of my time calling and visiting friends to tell them the good news. Pip was the first person that I telephoned. He was elated about the win and a lot more surprised than I expected. He had seen more of my flights than anyone else, and I sensed he didn't think I was really that good a flyer yet. In actuality, I probably wasn't that good the last time he saw me fly. Everything just seemed to come together at the competition when the pressure was on. After Pip congratulated me, I told him of my plans for the next flight.

By the time Saturday arrived, I was getting more than a little anxious about flying. It was a windy day as forecasted, so I set my sights on Sunday. If the weather predictions proved to be correct, then Sunday would be the perfect day for what I had in mind. In more ways than one.

Next to my home, is a small rectangular park which covers one city block. In the park, there are two fenced in baseball fields, one on each end. Between the ball fields, across the width of the park, was an open grass strip, which I estimated to be about four hundred feet long and eighty feet wide. On each end of the strip, there were small trees and power lines.

While standing in the park I made some rough calculations and figured that I could clear the power lines from either side by forty feet and still make a safe landing there. The distance from the airport was about eight miles by air. In a calm wind I could very easily make it a round trip. Bearing in mind that it is unacceptable to fly an ultralight aircraft over a populated area, I reasoned that I could fly along the rivers edge until I got there. The option to land in the park was intriguing and would make the flight special.

For as long as I could remember, I had wanted to see the area I grew up in, from up above. With this flight, I could accomplish that and more. I could also take photos of the area, giving me a permanent record of the first time I saw it by air. Previously, I had made the observation that the only time there were virtually no kids in the park was early on a Sunday morning, before 9:30 AM. My mind was made up that this would be my next flight and tomorrow would be the perfect day to do it, weather permitting.

Early on Saturday evening, I called Pip, told him of my plans and asked him to meet me at the airport at 7:00 AM. He agreed, and I called Mike and asked him if he could be there also, to take photos from the ground. He also agreed, so after getting everything prearranged, I settled down to get a good nights sleep. With my new found confidence, it was becoming much easier to sleep at night.

Upon arising at six in the morning, the first think I did was look out the window. The weather looked absolutely great. If it had been bad, I could have gone right back to bed. The night before, I told Pip and Mike I would call them if things looked good. That way, they didn't have to get up for nothing.

We all arrived at the airport within minutes of each other. Wasting no time, we removed the ParaPlane from the trailer and I gave it an extra good preflight because it had been folded and unfolded since I flew it last. Everything checked out good, so I filled my tank to the top and checked for wind direction. There was a very slight breeze out of the west. In no time flat, I had the craft running and pointed down the grass on the side of the cross runway.

During the engine warm up period, I decided that I was going to try landing in the park. While strapped into the seat, I told Pip and Mike to take my car and trailer, drive down to the side of the park and take some pictures of me coming in. Originally, I was only going to land there if my fuel supply was too low for the return trip. But I decided that if the flight was going to be a special one, I would have to land in the park.

Perhaps it was my new found confidence that caused me to be less nervous and more daring. In any event, although I was a little nervous, what I was feeling most was a rush of excitement. Flight number thirty three was about to go into the log book as one of the most unusual.

With my camera loaded and strapped to my belt, I flashed a thumbs up sign to my ground crew and pushed the throttle forward. The chute seemed to take forever to fill up with air. As I neared the point where I would have to abort the takeoff, the chute popped open and with a firm push to full throttle, I was in the air. The cool crisp morning air whistled through my helmet as I climbed up to my cruising altitude of eight hundred and fifty feet. Looking out over the river, I could see the reflection of the Braga Bridge in the still waters. In all my flights, I don't remember a calmer look to the Taunton River. It was just like the surface of a mirror.

Rock steady is the best way I can describe this flight. Air turbulence was nonexistent. And the view was nothing short of spectacular. Looking over the vast panorama, I felt as though I was observing a scale model of the city, complete in every possible detail. Little tiny cars driving over little tiny streets and stopping at little tiny red lights. The experience was so awe inspiring that I was beginning to lose track of time. I was becoming entranced, so I forced myself to concentrate on flying, in order to keep my mind on the task at hand.

Battleship Cove, Fall River, Mass.

Over the Battleship Cove area, I circled around once to get a longer birds-eye view. The cove consists of the Battleship Massachusetts, the Destroyer Kennedy and the Submarine Lionfish. These ships are open to the public, and I had visited them many times, but not from this unique vantage point.

The ParaPlane was performing beautifully in the still morning air. Heading along the shoreline, I found that I could easily stay on course by shifting my weight slightly. There was no need to use the steering arms. With the throttle set for level flight, I sat back with my arms and legs crossed and felt as though I was just along for the ride.

About twenty minutes had passed since I left the airport, and I was approaching my destination. All along the way, I had been taking pictures, but I was saving most of them for the end. As I circled around over my house, I took shot after shot. My excitement turned to frustration when I realized that I had taken over thirty pictures and the roll held only twenty four.

Two things were possible. Either the film roll actually held thirty six, or the film was improperly loaded on the take up reel. Since I remembered the roll to be a twenty four, it was more likely I loaded the film wrong. Especially since I loaded the camera in a hurry at the airport. There was no time for speculation now, I had to decide where I was going to land.

Pip and Mike had arrived at the park near my house. They were soon standing in the park awaiting my arrival. The gas tank was still more than half full. If I wanted to, I could still go back to the airport, although I would be cutting it close. Nervousness was beginning to replace the excitement of it all. I had to make a decision. I had to make it quick.

Wasting no time, I flew within sight of a huge, white, natural gas storage tank that had a florescent orange wind sock attached to the top railing. The sock was hanging completely limp. There was absolutely no detectable wind. Without a wind direction, I decided to pick the area that seemed to have the most room. As I flew back to the park, I dropped my altitude down to one hundred feet and made a low pass of the area from south to north. The spot I picked for a potential landing looked tiny until I made my low pass. Now, it looked more feasible.

People were starting to gather in the park to see what was going on. There was no time left for speculation. Soon the park would have too many people in it for me to make a safe landing attempt. I had to do it now or try to make it back to the airport while there was still enough fuel left. Even though I knew I was capable of this landing, my legs were shaking and my heart was pounding when I made the final decision to go for it.

Adding full throttle, I pushed the ParaPlane's right steering arm as hard as I could and banked around to line up for the landing. The last thing I wanted was to interface with a power line, so I purposely held my altitude a bit high as I approached the park.

The power lines were at least forty feet below me as I cleared them, and without hesitation, I pulled the throttle all the way back to idle in order to allow for the steepest drop rate possible. For the next few seconds, all I could do was wait.

Park landing approach.

Because there was no discernible wind, the ParaPlane dropped steadily on the parachute without requiring any steering corrections. As the craft reached the halfway point on the available landing area, it was still twenty feet off the ground. It was too late to abort the landing and there wasn't much park left to land on. Finally, with only about thirty feet of open grass area left in front of me, the ParaPlane touched down. Immediately, I pulled the throttle all the way back, stopping both engines. The cart kept rolling forward. I pushed both steering arms full forward to pull the chute down quicker for some added braking effect. The cart kept rolling forward.

The sidewalk at the end of the park was rapidly approaching. On the verge of panic, I started dragging my feet on the ground, but the cart kept on rolling forward. With every ounce of strength I could muster, I finally brought the ParaPlane to a complete stop on the sidewalk, just inches from a parked car.

The chute, still fully inflated, continued on and got hung up in the tree I passed under. Quickly, I exited the cart and with the help of my friends, pulled the chute out of the tree and packed it in its bag.

Many curious people were gathering around and I wanted to get the ParaPlane on its trailer and back in the garage as soon as possible to avoid having to confront the police. In seconds, I had the ParaPlane rolling down the street and into the driveway.

Before I could get it back in the garage though, the police stopped in front of my driveway. They sat in the car and stared at me standing in front of the ParaPlane. I stared back. Not a word was spoken. After a minute or so, they slowly drove away with a kind of puzzled look on their faces. It seemed as though they just didn't know what to say. After all, what do you say to a guy who lands a strange looking craft in a city park?

What are the legal implications? My guess is that because nothing was damaged and no one complained, they decided to leave well enough alone.

Flight number 33 was now history. Although I didn't know it at the time, a slight tail wind had developed upon landing causing me to use up more ground area than I anticipated and pushing the chute into the trees. The flight could have been more of a disaster because I failed to allow enough room for error. Only now, was I beginning to realize that I still had a lot to learn about flying a powered parachute.

Later that Sunday, I checked my camera and found that all the snapshots that I thought I had taken, did not exist. The film had not been loaded correctly. If I wanted to have some pictures of the area I grew up in, it looked as though the flight would have to be repeated. Fortunately, Mike took some photos from the ground and so did my next door neighbor, Paul Fournier, so at least I had a record of the flight.

With my confidence somewhat shattered, I spent the week waiting for ideal weather conditions, which never arose. The weekend started out with a less than perfect Saturday, so when Sunday arrived I was getting more than a little anxious. It had been a full week since I last flew and I needed to prove to myself that I was still a capable flier.

Sunday morning was a bit windy and when I talked to Pip on the phone, he recommended that I wait for a calmer day. He was probably right, but I decided to go for it anyway since my friend from work, Marc Leclair, was available to help me out, along with Pip and Danny. Also, I wanted to fly out of Myricks Field.

On my 26th flight, I had flown **to** Myricks, but I never flew **from** there. The strip runs east-west but a ParaPlane could take off north-south if the conditions warranted it. It's a minimum field for a south-north takeoff due to a row of tall trees along the north edge, which would cause mechanical turbulence of the wind and a lot of sink when you're trying to climb. Nevertheless, I was very anxious to fly, so I rounded everyone up and we arrived at Myricks by mid-morning.

The wind was strong, blowing at about 10 miles per hour, with gusts up to 20, but it was out of the west giving me plenty of room, so I decided to fly. Pip thought I was crazy.

He pointed out that the wind was not only too strong, it was shifting. Nevertheless, I told him that I could handle it because, I was the official ParaPlane "WORLD CHAMPION!"

For some strange reason, my confidence was at a very high level. It was probably due to the fact that I was feeling very good physically. It couldn't have been from my last flight, although even though it was far from perfect, I did manage to pull it off without any dire consequences.

Pip went along with me somewhat reluctantly and we set the ParaPlane up in the grass facing west. No sooner did I remove the chute from the bag, when a gust of wind caught it and we had all we could do to hold the ParaPlane from taking off all by itself. With a considerable amount of effort, Pip, Marc, Danny and I pulled the chute down and held it on the ground. The wind was really starting to blow and it was shifting direction from west to north and back again.

Now, I was beginning to have second thoughts. Without Pip and Danny holding the chute, I never would have been able to even consider flying. However, with their help, I was able to start the engines and strap myself in the cart. I didn't want to abort the flight. I reasoned that if I waited until the wind was steady out of the west, I would be able to take off without any problem.

For about ten minutes, I sat in the cart and waited. The wind showed no signs of abating. For a few minutes, it would blow out of the north. Then very abruptly, it would shift to the west. After this cycle repeated itself a few times, I thought I had a shot at catching the wind at the right moment.

Pip and Danny were struggling with the chute, trying to hold it on the ground against its will. It wanted to kite up and fly, as if it had a mind of its own. Knowing that they wouldn't be able to hold on to it much longer, I readied myself to go on the next wind shift to the west.

Suddenly, the wind shifted to the northwest, and figuring it would soon be west, I signaled my weary wing holders to let go. Immediately, as they released their grips on the fabric, the chute blasted into the sky above me. To prevent the cart from being dragged backwards, I had to apply at least three quarters throttle. This produced enough thrust to cause the cart to begin lifting off the ground, and I had to jockey the throttle back and forth to hold my position. The chute was oscillating from side to side in the shifting wind and I should have aborted my flight attempt, but my stupid pride wouldn't let me. Violent gyrations were setting up in the chute, and I strained my neck muscles to keep a constant watch on its varying position overhead. For a split second, it seemed that the chute had finally stabilized in the right position, directly overhead.   Without hesitation, I pushed the throttle to start my ground roll. It required almost full throttle, just to start the cart rolling.

The next few seconds seemed like hours as the cart reluctantly crept forward and began to lift.   Suddenly, the wind shifted ninety degrees and the chute was now on the left side of the cart and beginning to pull the cart over. I pulled the throttle back to idle and with all the strength I could muster, I tried to hold the cart upright by extending my left leg to the side. For an instant, it seemed like I was winning, but the wind was relentless and my strength was waning, so I killed the engines and pulled my weary left leg back onto the cart.

Before I was able to get my body into a tucked position, the cart rolled over and I was hanging upside down! Flustered but unhurt, I could see the inverted figures of my friends as they ran towards me to offer their assistance. I tried releasing the seat belt, but the weight of my body seemed to be preventing it from disengaging. All I could think about for the couple of minutes it took them to free me, was how foolish I must have looked to them. What a moron I was! No doubt about it, I let my pride force me to make an error in judgement that could have had serious consequences. How could I possibly think that

I was a good enough pilot to overcome the powerful forces of nature? Especially since only a few months ago, I wouldn't fly even if there was a whisper of wind? My confidence was shattered, my ego deflated.

Standing beside my overturned aircraft and realizing my stupidity, I resolved to let this most humbling experience become a firm lesson in how very important the rules are when it comes to piloting a ParaPlane, or any plane. You can never be too careful.

Although I was shook up, I came away from this experience without a scratch. The ParaPlane, however, did not fare as well. Fortunately, the only damage was a broken fiberglass guide post. The propellors were undamaged, thanks to my shutting off the engines when I realized that a rollover was imminent. However, even if there had been no damage, there's no way I would have attempted another flight under such adverse wind conditions. Flight number thirty four would have to wait for a while. I thought about an old saying as we packed up to go home. "I would rather be on the ground wishing I was in the air, than in the air wishing I was on the ground." That old axiom was taking on a new meaning. The clouds that enveloped my head since the competition, were beginning to clear away.

On October seventh, nine days later, I met Pip at the airport for my first flight since the rollover. With a converted fishing pole to replace the broken fiberglass rod, I was a little nervous about flying. Nevertheless, conditions were extremely good, and I performed a very thorough pre-flight examination, so nervous or not, I knew I could get a flight in.

Even though the weather seemed ideal, when you're dealing with ultralight flying, circumstances can change at a moment's notice. This excerpt from my flight log, best describes what happened. "FIRST FLIGHT AFTER SUNDAY ROLLOVER AT MYRICKS - SHIFTING WINDS - SLID ONTO RUNWAY - TURNED NORTH - LIFTED OFF

SHORT OF TREES - SOME NERVOUSNESS - GOOD
LANDING."

Another lesson learned. Upon takeoff, the wind shifted
and made for some very anxious moments. This time, though, I
was prepared for it and made all the necessary corrections for a
safe liftoff. While it is true that I could (some would say
should) have aborted the takeoff attempt, at no time did I feel
out of control or incapable of succeeding. If in fact the situation became any more threatening, I felt a new confidence that
I would make the correct decision and abort the attempt, if
necessary. This flight was a milestone of sorts for me. A new
confidence based on maximum respect for flying was giving me
the strength I needed to become a truly proficient pilot.

Within the next few weeks of October, I logged seven more
breathtakingly beautiful flights. My flying buddy Gene and I
flew after work one evening, staying in the air until dusk. Floating rock steady at about eight hundred feet, we were mesmerized by the sight of the setting sun reflecting off the still
waters of the Taunton River. We watched intently as the cloud
laced orange disc melted slowly into the horizon, converting the
twilight into darkness.

Neither of us wanted to land that night. We stayed aloft
for the full half hour allowed after sunset. The runway lights
were lit when we finally decided to touch down and conclude a
most enjoyable flight.

Six days passed until my next flight, which I accomplished
alone and without fanfare. Then, two days later, I managed to
put together a string of five flights on a daily basis.

On each of these flights, something different occurred
which furthered my knowledge of the changing complexities of
weather. First I had to deal with a fairly strong wind of about
twelve miles per hour, which picked up during the flight, forcing

me to land in it. There was some difficulty getting the chute down, but other than that, the flight was a good one.

The following night, while flying back to the airport I encountered some kind of a wind shift which bounced the cart and spun me sideways. The effect was short lived but quite severe. Although the turbulence abated and the rest of the flight was smooth, I wasted no time getting my feet back on the ground.

During the next two flights, the only minor difficulty that I encountered was a bouncy air mass near the ground, making for a tricky and somewhat hard touchdown. These landings were a good experience and only served to sharpen my reflexes.

On the last of this series of flights, I decided to take some photos of a house owned by a friend of mine in the east end of the city. The house is located on the edge of the watershed, allowing me free access without flying over a populated area to get there. Wind conditions were as close to perfect as possible when I lifted off.

Using only weight shift to steer, it took me half an hour to reach the house. After exhausting a roll of film, I headed back to the airport with half a tank of gas and a slight tail wind. When I reached the airport with very little fuel left, I immediately lined up to land in the area I took off from. The flight was a long one and very smooth. I was thinking about the beauty of the surrounding countryside, and as I dropped to within fifty feet of the ground, I noticed that I was going sideways!

Foolishly, I didn't bother to look at the wind sock and just assumed the wind was still out of the same direction as when I took off. With just enough altitude left to abort the landing, I pushed the throttle full forward and swung around for another landing attempt. A glance at the wind sock told the story. What little wind there was had shifted a full ninety degrees. Shaking off my euphoria, I aimed the ParaPlane into the wind and executed a perfect three point gentle landing.

Ironically, the flight had been so enjoyable that I allowed my attention span to wander almost to the point of a potential accident. Although the ParaPlane is equipped with caster type rear landing gear, designed for slight crosswind landings, a ninety degree crosswind would almost surely tip the cart over on touchdown. If a rollover had occurred, because of the slow speed of the craft, most likely my pride would have suffered the most damage because a mishap of this type would surely have to be classified as pilot error.

Every new flight, no matter how routine it seemed, was bringing with it a greater feeling of confidence in my capabilities as a flier. I didn't know it at the time, but my very next flight was going to test my abilities to the absolute limit.

In upstate New York, there was a ParaPlane dealer that had organized a flight competition. Gene and I had both received a copy of their brochure in the mail a few weeks prior to the event and we were looking forward to attending. "Come fly with us in the beautiful Mohawk Valley," their booklet enticed.

It seemed like a wonderful idea, the Mohawk Valley area in the autumn with the brilliant splendor of the turning leaves was a draw in itself. We could bring along our cameras and get some great shots of a crimson wonderland. There was to be plenty of cross country flying, coupled with a spirited competition.

Our plan was to break down both our ParaPlanes and fit them into the back of my pickup truck. Since my truck has a small bed, four by six feet, I designed a rack made of two pieces of lumber to allow us to fit the two power systems in the rear, one on top of the other. This would leave ample room for both of our airframes, side by side. Gas cans and tools could take up the remaining space. We could share expenses and ride together in one vehicle, thereby having the time during the three to four hour drive to discuss our plans for the weekend.

On the Friday before the event, after I had loaded everything I needed into my truck, I spoke with Gene on the telephone. He assured me that he was all packed and ready to meet me at five o'clock in the morning. We discussed our travel plans and ended the conversation with intentions to get to bed early.

That evening upon retiring, I laid in bed and entertained thoughts of what possible scenarios could occur in the days ahead. Most likely the competition would be fun and I felt strongly that there would be an excellent chance I could win some part of it. Even if the weather conditions weren't right for competing, I was really looking forward to partaking in the planned cross country flying events. As I pictured a squadron of ParaPlanes soaring over the multi-colored landscape, I had no trouble at all falling asleep.

Never in my wildest dreams could I have imagined the terror that awaited me. If I had known what was in store for me, insomnia would have ruled the night.

CHAPTER 8

FRIGHT FLIGHTS

An exciting event was about to take place, and for the first time, I was asleep when the alarm rang. It felt great to have gotten a full night's sleep and when Gene arrived, I was ready and eager to get on the road. After a few minutes of rearranging things in the truck to accommodate both ParaPlanes, we loaded up and headed for upstate New York.

On the turnpike, we paused for breakfast. As we walked from the truck to the restaurant, we commented to each other that there were exceptionally calm wind conditions. If we were at the field already, we could have flown without any problem.

Soon we were back on the highway and within a few hours of driving, our exit approached, and we left the interstate for the back roads. With Gene playing navigator, I drove through a series of small towns and about a mile after crossing the Mohawk River, we approached our destination.

On the right side of the roadway in a valley along the river, stood a fairly large white hangar that was attached to a couple of aging hangars that were in a sad state of disrepair. There were sections of wall missing and massive holes in the roof. The main hangar was in pretty good shape and we parked the truck on the side of it. Looking out over the field, I could see no sign of any paved landing strip, just a lot of rolling grass. It was a perfect spot for flying a ParaPlane.

Gene and I stepped out of the truck and stood for a minute, stretching our legs and drinking in the colorful scenery. All around the valley there were mountains dressed in multicolored foliage. It was a breathtaking sight and I was looking forward to taking some pictures from both the ground and above.

Realizing that it was now almost noon and the wind was picking up, we decided not to waste any more time and walked around to the front of the hangar. The door was wide open and inside were two men working on a ParaPlane. All around them stood a number of other ParaPlanes. Gene and I strolled in and introduced ourselves.

As we shook hands, they told us their names were Stewart Cavanaugh and Dennis Fancher. Stewart, the shorter of the two, ran the operation. He came across as a very strong willed person who seemed to fear nothing. He told us of his exploits flying aerobatics in fixed wing ultralights at air shows. He spoke with an air of confidence, and I was anxious to see him fly.

Dennis was a reserved individual. He was tall, wiry, and spoke very little, but it was obvious that he loved flying. Soon after meeting him, I realized that I had seen him before. He had attended the competition in New Jersey. I remembered him as one of the winners. He had won second place in the bomb drop category, the only division that I failed in. It was good to see him again after so long.

Stewart was explaining the rules of the planned competition when I spotted another person I recognized. It was a man named John Murphy, who I had also met at the competition. John didn't win anything as I recall, but he was a person who was hard to forget. Known to his friends as "Big John", he was a tall strapping man who had developed a reputation for hard landings. That a man of his size and weight could even fly a ParaPlane, truly amazed me. Although he cut an imposing figure, John was a gentle man, the type who would give you the shirt off his back. Gene and I were glad he showed up.

Before long, morning turned into afternoon, and just as we were all assembled and ready to fly in the competitive events, the wind picked up and put a damper on the activities. As anyone who has ever flown any ultralight knows, you learn to accept the bad days and find something else to do. We spent the rest of the day getting acquainted, and fine tuning our respective aircraft. Although the dealership had sent out plenty of invitations, only the five of us had shown up by the end of the day. My thinking was that it must have been due to a less than perfect weekend weather forecast.

Soon the setting sun eliminated our chances of flying for the day, so we stored our ParaPlanes in the hangar, and Gene and I headed to a local motel for the night. Stewart had suggested that all of us meet at a restaurant for supper and to discuss our plans for the next day. Everyone agreed, so after Gene and I checked into the motel, we met the others at a little eatery on the outskirts of town.

After we finished our meal, it was unanimously agreed upon to meet early in the morning for a cross country flight.

Stewart explained that if we flew our cross country in the morning, perhaps more people would show up by afternoon, allowing for a far more spirited competition. For the cross country, Dennis' wife was to meet us at predetermined fields along the way, where we could land, refuel and continue on. The plan was to try to cover fifty miles.

It sounded like an exciting trek, and I could hardly wait to get started. Gene seemed as excited as I was and also very anxious. He and I both expressed the opinion that the cross country events were the most fun. We figured that because we were unfamiliar with the area we would be flying in, we could simply follow the others. There should be no problem finding our way. Everything sounded great. It sounded terrific. If we only knew what awaited us, we wouldn't have been in such a happy mood. If we only knew.

The night was getting old, and we were all very eager to fly in the morning so we broke up the party, and headed for our respective sleeping quarters. I remember worrying about getting enough sleep for an early start, but for some reason, I slept like a log. When the alarm awoke us at five in the morning, I opened my eyes to total darkness. Sleepily peering out of the motel window, all I could discern was that it was calm and not raining. We wasted no time getting ready and heading to a diner for breakfast.

For whatever reason, although it was probably due to the excitement, I was more nervous than usual. Gene seemed unusually tense also. We joked around a lot during breakfast, probably just to relieve some of the tension. The food was good and plentiful, but my appetite wasn't up to par. Gene was less than famished also, so we left half our food, quickly paid the tab, and scrambled out of the diner. It was obvious that we were teething at the bit with anticipation.

When we arrived at the field, Stewart, Dennis and "Big John" were waiting for us. It seemed like a perfect day for flying. Although the rising sun hadn't crested the mountains yet, the sky was clear. There was only a slight breeze out of the north. Stewart briefed us thoroughly on the flight plans and weather forecast. He told us they were predicting moderate low level turbulence to occur around noon time. Moderate turbulence can toss a good sized airplane around, he had explained, but we should have time to fly at least a couple of legs of the cross country. It sounded logical to me. As soon as it started to get a little windy, we could land and head back to home base.

We pushed our ParaPlanes down to the far end of the field. It was decided that because of his weight, Big John would take off first to give him a head start. This would give him time to climb up to the twelve hundred feet necessary to clear the mountain ridge. Over the ridge, the land leveled off towards the west, which was our intended direction.

Big John strapped himself in and headed down the grass runway. After what seemed like three times the distance that I would have needed for takeoff, John lifted off and began to climb, ever so slowly. I shook my head in disbelief that he could even fly the thing, at his weight.

During the wait, we did a thorough pre-flight examination and warmed up our engines. Then, one by one, the remaining four of us took to the skies. It didn't take us long to catch up to Big John, who seemed to know where he was going, as he headed out over the ridge.

Behind me, the valley was about thirteen hundred feet below, but the land over the crest of the first mountain was only about four hundred feet below. I took a last look at the splendor of the valley as I crossed the ridge. My camera was with me, but I didn't have time to take a picture of the area. The others were getting ahead of me, and because I'm lighter and fly a little bit slower, I didn't want to take any chance of losing sight of them.

The scenery was magnificent and it seemed to be even more colorful ahead of us, so I figured there was plenty of time for taking pictures later. As we flew over the flat land above the valley, I could see row after row of colorful mountains to the north. To the south, the land seemed to slope gently away from us and ahead to the west, the terrain appeared to be heavily forested with rolling hills. Quaint little farm houses sporadically dotted the landscape in every direction. Cows could be seen grazing lazily in the open fields.

So far, partly due to my unfamiliarity with the area, this cross country was evolving as one of the most enjoyable on record for me. At the time, I could not think of one thing that might spoil it. The vivid, glorious colors of the trees brought to mind an old song, and I began to sing it aloud. "The...autumn...leaves...caress the trees...tenderly." Tenderly, yes, but believe me, not for long.

About four hundred feet in front of me, and to the left, was Gene. About half a mile in front of him I could see Big John. He was obviously flying a few miles an hour faster than the rest of us, due to his extra weight. To the north, on my right about one eighth of a mile away was Stewart, with Dennis a few hundred feet behind him.

We were about twenty minutes into the flight, which so far was quite smooth, when I began to notice a little turbulence. At this point, the scenery was especially beautiful, so not being overly concerned about a few bumps, I decided to remove the camera from my pocket.

The camera strap was wrapped around my belt for safety purposes. Following the strap with my hand, I began to pull the camera from my right side pants pocket. Before I had retracted it halfway, a strong jolt startled me, and I let the camera go and grabbed hold of the seat. After a few seconds of bouncing around, the winds calmed a bit, so I released my hand grip on the seat, and pushed the camera back into my pocket. Under these conditions, I decided to wait a while to take photos.

Without warning, the bouncing started again and this time, I grabbed for the outrigger arms and held on tight. In all my flights, I had never experienced wind turbulence that even came close to these conditions. The cart was starting to oscillate back and forth as well as up and down. Terror was beginning to come over me as I fought to maintain control of a three hundred pound flying machine that was dangling from strings hundreds of feet in the air.

I wondered if the others were going through the same kind of trauma that I was experiencing. Looking over at Stewart, I could see his cart swinging wildly. It was pitching forward and then backward, swinging so far forward that the front of the cart was level with the leading edge of his chute! Behind him, Dennis was flying lower and also gyrating wildly. Big John was so far ahead it was difficult to see what was happening to him, but Gene was only a few hundred feet in front of me and flying very low. It seemed like he was trying to get under the gusting winds, but was having little success. His canopy was ruffling wildly like a flag in a heavy wind. He came so close to a row of power lines that I remember screaming at the top of my lungs for him to add throttle. Although I knew he couldn't hear me, I continued to scream as loud as I could because it seemed to have a controlling effect on me. The primal outbursts must have eased my mind somewhat and given me a feeling of confidence--or perhaps I yelled out of sheer terror!

Fighting with the steering arms and throttle, I tried to maintain my position behind Gene, but the cart was turning of its own accord. When I pushed in on a steering arm to correct my course, the arm would go all the way to the stop with no resistance as if it were disconnected from the chute steering lines. It took every bit of effort I could muster to try and keep the craft flying in one direction. It seemed to have a will of its own. At one point, the ParaPlane did a complete one hundred and eighty degree turn, all by itself, and headed in the opposite direction!

I could not believe what was happening. I had to release my hand hold on the outrigger arms, because the chute support cables were rocking so far back and forth that they were crushing my hands. My arms and legs were flailing around searching for something to attach to. The only thing holding me in was the glorious seat belt, and I prayed to God it would not let go and dump me into oblivion.

For a few minutes, which seemed more like an eternity, I felt like I was just along for the ride. No matter what I did, it didn't seem to matter. The ParaPlane was doing whatever the diabolical wind wanted it to. It felt like my life was literally hanging by a thread. Hanging by a thread, and there was absolutely nothing I could do about it. The gripping feeling of helplessness was almost overpowering. I closed my eyes and tried to convince myself that I could get through this, if only the craft would hold together.

Little by little, I began to regain marginal control of the Para-Plane. Whenever the gyrating would lessen, I would add full throttle to restore any lost altitude. When the fluctuations became uncontrollable, I dropped power to an idle and let the natural pendulum stability of the ParaPlane restore some equilibrium.

My tactics seemed to be effective. Ever so slowly my confidence was returning. Then all of a sudden it felt as though the proverbial thread had broken! The cart tipped on its side, and started to freefall as if all of the support lines had been torn away from the chute. In about two seconds, the craft dropped about sixty feet, sideways! My heart was in my mouth, and I thought for sure it was the end of the line this time. But just as suddenly as the fall began, the little cart abruptly swung from right to left wildly, and began to stabilize. I let out a blood curdling scream, and pushed the throttle full forward to regain the hundred feet of altitude I had lost in just a few seconds!

I had no idea what had happened to cause the drop, but I was sure elated to still be flying. After a bouncy climb back up to four hundred feet, I looked over to see where Stewart and Dennis were. Scanning the sky to the north, I could see no sign of them. They must have gone down somewhere while I was fighting to remain airborne. Ahead of me, Gene was still flying and maintaining only about a hundred feet of altitude. There was no sign of Big John at all.

Still struggling with the relentless gusts of wind, I kept a sharp eye on Gene. Besides myself, he was the only one still aloft, and I didn't want to lose sight of him. He was down to about fifty feet now, and it appeared he was lining up for an emergency landing in a farmer's cow field.

The field was quite huge, and separated into two sections by a stone wall. Black and white cows were grazing in small groups throughout the foot tall grass. Gene was trying to get to a clear section of the field, but he was bouncing around so much, he was having trouble reaching it. Finally, during a rare lull in the wind, he plopped onto the field.

From my precarious perch at two hundred feet, I watched as Gene struggled to pull his chute down in the unyielding wind. As I suspected would happen, the wind gusts were so powerful that he was unable to hold the cart in position. The chute dragged his cart backwards and flipped it over on the props. He had shut down the engines before he tipped over, probably preventing any damage to the blades, and from what I could see, he was unhurt.

Lying on his back in the seat, Gene unbuckled his seat belt and rolled out onto the ground. I envied him. His ordeal was over. He was safe and sound on good old mother earth. His ParaPlane was all through flying for the day. Fortunately, it seems that when a ParaPlane cart tips over backwards, it automatically pulls the chute down by its inherent design, and you don't get dragged any further.

Gene stood in the field brushing himself off and looked up at me. He appeared to be trying to signal me. I was hoping he was thinking what I was thinking. If I could land near him, he could grab hold of the front of my cart and maybe prevent me from tipping over as he had done.

My altitude was now down to ninety feet, but the ride was still like a roller coaster. I was hovering over the field just before the one Gene had landed it, and trying in vain to reach him. The stone wall that separated the two fields was just ahead of me, but I couldn't seem to clear it. Every time I would make a little progress towards it, a gust of wind would blow me back again. I knew that if I wanted to make any headway, I would have to lower my altitude. Slowly, I let the ParaPlane sink towards the ground, and at forty feet, I began to inch forward.

At this altitude, there was no room for error. A weird wind gust could throw me into the ground.

When I finally reached the field Gene was in, I maneuvered the ParaPlane as best as I could toward him, and as I hovered over him, I chopped the throttle back and dropped straight down like a helicopter. It was definitely not one of my better landings.

Gene grabbed hold of the front of the cart as I had hoped he would, and figuring he could hold it in place, I killed the engines. That was probably not such a good idea. With the wind still gusting, the chute began to drag the cart backwards even with Gene holding on to it. What I should have done was pull on a steering line to bring the chute down, but in my panicky state of mind, I tried to hold the cart back by dragging my feet. The wind was so strong that we were both being dragged backwards by the four hundred square foot canopy. I was determined not to let the cart flip over. I dug my feet into the ground so hard that my shoes and socks came off! The ParaPlane kept on moving backward. Gene's knuckles were turning white from the strain, but he held on tight. My bare feet were being dragged through the slippery grass when I felt them hit something soft and mushy. It was cow dung! This was a cow field and it was full of cow manure! My feet were covered with crap when we were finally able to bring the Para-Plane to a stop without it flipping over.

The great relief of being back on solid ground with no ill effects was overwhelming. I would have kissed the ground had it not been so inundated with cow flop. In short order, we packed our chutes, and began pushing our flying machines up the sloping field toward the farm house.

Off in the distance we could hear the sound of sirens increasing in intensity as if they were getting closer and closer. As we lifted our gaze toward the farm house, we could see a lot of flashing lights that spread out along the approaching roadway.

There were fire engines, police cars and rescue wagons arriving in droves! They all stopped at the farm house, and soon a group of paramedics (no pun intended) were scurrying down the field in our direction. Realizing at this point that we were the reason they came, I looked over at Gene and said, "I think we're in trouble." We had no idea why they were interested in us, but it didn't take us long to find out.

They wanted to know if we were hurt in any way. It seemed that someone in the vicinity had reported that there must have been a plane crash, because they saw two parachutes coming down! The paramedics were expecting to find the occupants of a downed airplane. They had never seen a Para-Plane before.

It took some explaining on our part, but once they understood about the type of craft we were flying they were very congenial. They weren't upset, just relieved that we were not hurt. Actually, they were quite fascinated with the ParaPlane, and after asking many questions about the capabilities of the craft, they even helped us push our ParaPlanes out of the cow field. We thanked them for their concern, and soon they were on their way.

Gene and I were both physically and emotionally exhausted from our ordeal, but happy we were still in one piece. He had a couple of bruises from his flip over, but no major injuries. I emerged without a scratch, thanks to Gene. Without his help, there was no way I would have been able to keep the cart upright. Our problems were far from over, though. Here we were stranded in a cow field in upstate New York, and we had no idea of our exact location, nor any evident means of transportation.

The farm house, as it turned out, was owned by an older gent who was very accommodating, although somewhat crusty. He allowed us to use his telephone, and I called the airfield, hoping against hope that someone might be there. After about thirty rings, I relented and hung up the phone.

Stewart and Dennis were probably stranded in fields as we were, so there would be no one to answer the phone at the airfield and it was the only number we had available to call. Big John, I felt, was our only hope. Since he was so far ahead of us, there was a slim chance he may have made it to our first intended refueling stop. He would then have a ride back to the airfield, allowing us to reach somebody.

After thanking the farmer for the use of his phone, I rejoined Gene who was keeping an eye on the ParaPlanes outside. We talked it over, and concluded that all we could do at this point was wait and keep on trying to call the airfield.

The minutes seemed like hours as we milled around outside the farm. Trying to kill time, I ventured around the yard and spotted something inside an old barn that gave me an idea. It was a bicycle. As fast as I could run, I raced up to the farmer and asked him if I could borrow the bicycle to ride back to the airfield. This would allow me to return in the truck, pick up the ParaPlanes, and return the bicycle. The farmer thought for a minute, then reluctantly said I could use the bike.

Gene agreed to stay with the aircraft and wait for my return. The farmer gave me some insight into what direction to go in, and after stuffing my pant leg into my sock, I headed for the barn. But before I took two steps out of the barn with the shiny new bike, the farmer stopped me.

"Not that one," he said. "That's my son's new one, take the one in back of it." Behind the new bike was a beat up old balloon tire relic that had seen better days.

"You've got to be kidding!" I exclaimed. "The tires are half flat and the front wheel is coming loose."

"Take it or leave it," he said bluntly.

There was no reasoning with this man. Grudgingly, I dragged the dust laden, rusted, poor excuse for a bicycle out of the barn.

It had been a long time since I had ridden a bike this old. It was a single speed with foot brakes. I was used to riding a lightweight ten speed bicycle. Nevertheless, brushing the dust off the seat, I threw myself over the bar, and waved goodbye to Gene and the farmer as I pedaled out of the driveway and down the hill.

Halfway down the hill, the front wheel started to oscillate uncontrollably, so I applied the brakes. There weren't any! I was blasting down a steep grade with a loose front wheel and no brakes! I don't know how I did it, but I managed to stay on the bike all the way down the hill at about forty miles an hour, and right through an intersection with a stop sign. This was not my idea of a good time. Perhaps I should have checked the bike over more thoroughly, but---who would ever think you would have to pre-flight a bicycle? Fortunately, there were no more big downhills.

At every intersection, I had to remember the turns in order to find my way back. About thirty five miles of hard pedaling later, I spotted the airfield. The tires on the bike were almost completely flat and I was physically exhausted when I reached the entrance to the airfield.

From the bumpy dirt access road, I could see that Stewart and Dennis had found their way back, and were unloading their ParaPlanes from Dennis' pickup truck. They watched with puzzled looks on their faces as I pedaled over to them on a bicycle that looked like it was resurrected from a scrap yard.

"Hi guys!" I bellowed cheerfully.

They shook their heads in disbelief and said in unison:

"We can't **wait** to hear **your** story!"

Briefly, I explained to them what had happened to us, and then asked them for their account of what happened. Dennis said that he decided to land the minute it got uncontrollably bumpy. Stewart, although he considered remaining aloft a bit longer, saw Dennis go down, and opted to follow him in. They ended up in separate fields, but were near enough to one another to establish contact. Without a cart holder, both of them flipped over backwards, slightly damaging the propellor shrouds, and snapping off a fiberglass guide rod. They walked to a house and called Dennis' wife, who came to pick them up. They didn't have to wait long.

"Where is Big John?" I asked.

"He called a few minutes ago, Stewart said, you wouldn't believe where he ended up! We're heading out to pick him up right now. Want to come along?"

"I wouldn't miss this for the world!" I said. "Let's pick up Gene first, he'd like to go along, too."

Soon after, we hitched up a trailer to Dennis' truck, and they followed me out to pick up Gene. When we arrived, Gene was relieved and happy to see us. We put his ParaPlane in Dennis' truck, and put mine in my truck, saving the trailer for Big John. We were all anxious to see where he had set down. According to Stewart, John had to land in someone's back yard!

Following Dennis and Stewart in my truck, we drove for about twenty-five minutes over winding roads, and left the rural countryside, heading into a heavily wooded area. The road narrowed and for miles, all you could see were trees. Finally, we reached a narrow intersecting road, and just around the corner in the middle of a dense forest stood one lonely house. We pulled into the driveway.

Big John met us halfway up the walk. There was no sign of his ParaPlane. And there was no sign of any area big enough to land a ParaPlane! John asked us to follow him behind the house. As we headed for the back yard, I looked up at the numerous very tall trees that surrounded the house, and I could not imagine anyone being able to land anywhere near here.

Then we saw it. Smack in the middle of what I estimated to be a forty foot square area stood John's ParaPlane, leaning to the side with its front wheel broken off. There was less than half an inch of gas in the tank. Big John told us that he had flown as far as possible with the gas he had available, and still he could see nothing but trees. Then out of nowhere he spotted a tiny little house, with a tiny little back yard. Realizing he had no choice, he skimmed over the roof of the house, pushed both steering arms to stall the chute, and dropped precariously into the tiny back yard without hitting anything, and all this in a strong gusting wind!

It was an incredible feat. The only damage to the cart was the front wheel. He walked away without a scratch! Big John generally hits the ground hard anyway. He was known for destroying front wheels. You might say for him it was a normal landing. Still, none of us could believe the tiny area he landed in.

He further related to us that when he came over the roof of the house, a woman was standing in the back yard smiling and waving to him. She had no idea he was attempting an emergency landing. He was thankful she didn't stand in the middle of the yard. To this day, she probably thinks it was an ordinary flight. I don't believe any of us told her otherwise. There wasn't any point in causing her undue concern. We said goodbye to the lady after loading John's ParaPlane, and she smiled and wished us well.

We arrived back at the airfield by late in the afternoon. There was still a considerable amount of daylight left. Stewart and Dennis, although I would have expected them to shun flying for a while after what happened, seemed anxious to fly before dark. They quickly repaired their damaged aircraft, and headed out into the open field. Since I hadn't any damage on my aircraft, it would have been possible for me to join them. However, after the traumatic experience of the morning, I wasn't sure that I wanted to.

The weather was pretty decent, there was still a bit of wind blowing, but it was nothing compared to the morning gale. I thought it over, and decided to go for it. As soon as I made the commitment to take to the sky, I became extremely nervous. Second thoughts raced through my mind. It was then that I realized how strong an impact the morning's flight had made on me. I was really, really scared. In fact, I was actually trembling at the thought of another flight.

As much as I wanted to stay on the ground, a part of me wanted to fly. I felt that if I didn't fly as soon as possible, I would never fly again. It was something that I <u>had</u> to do. If I had let any of my initial fears stop me on my first flight, I would never have had all of the wonderful experiences of personal flight. Darkness would be upon us soon, there was no time for procrastination.

Still shaking, I started pushing my aircraft out into the field. It was cold and damp, and the sky had taken on an eerie glow. The huge mountains surrounding the valley appeared as ominous shadows in the dwindling daylight. My stomach was full of butterflies as it was, I didn't need any help from the creepy surrounding area.

To shake off the jitters, I actually ran as hard as I could while pushing the ParaPlane to a clear, open takeoff spot. Huffing and puffing, I aligned the craft with the wind line, opened up the chute, pre-flighted, and started the engines. It felt good to sit in the seat and try to relax, while waiting for the engines to warm up.

Stewart and Dennis were already flying and making passes at the ribbons that were set up for the flight competition, the one that never materialized. They seemed to be at ease and having fun. It was time for me to join them.

Slowly, I edged the throttle forward, and the flapping bundle of nylon cloth behind me fluttered into the sky over my head, magically turned into a wing and lifted me into the twilight. I was flying again! It felt wonderful to be back in the air, and as I floated majestically over the field, I felt my fears melting away and my confidence returning. I joined up with the others, making practice runs over the ribbons.

The air was still a little turbulent, making it difficult to fly with any accuracy. After a few rough passes, we all landed gently, and headed back to the hangar. The flight was exactly what I needed. My spirit was renewed and I knew I would have no trouble flying again. Back at the hangar, Gene asked me how it felt to fly again after getting "scared to death."

"Not so good at first," I told him, "but great once I got back into it. I'm really glad I did it."

I sensed that he wished he had flown also, but he was in no hurry to fix his aircraft, and I'm sure the morning "terror flight" had a lot to do with it.

It was dark and the five of us were famished. We packed up quickly, left the field and met at a local eatery. During the meal, each of us took turns deftly narrating our versions of the morning's fright flight. Big John was in the air the longest, and his story was the most amazing. He had less of a problem with the turbulence, though, because of his increased weight. Everyone had an interesting tale to tell, but the thing that had the biggest impression on me was the fear that the apparently "fearless" Stewart revealed.

"I've been flying ultralights for years," he said. "All types of flying; aerobatics, upside down, you name it. But I've never been as scared as I was today."

It was sobering to hear him admit his terror.

"The main reason for my fear," he went on, "was the help-less feeling of not being in control."

I could not have agreed more. During the height of the strong turbulence, we were all nothing more than "puppets on a string", destined to ride the cyclonic whirlwinds until a greater power decided our fate. We were all at the mercy of the awesome power of nature.

Stewart went on to say, "John, if you had seen what happened to your chute, you would have landed immediately! I just happened to be looking over at you bouncing around, when I saw your chute collapse! It must have gotten hit by an extra strong gust at one point, because it folded up like an accordion, and it looked like you lost it."

"That must have been when I free-fell about sixty feet," I said, "It felt like all the chute lines were ripped away, but the cart finally stabilized and I regained limited control."

I never told them that I was screaming at the top of my lungs! My guess is, I was not the only one who was screaming.

There was one thing that we all agreed on, though. It's doubtful that a fixed wing ultralight could have survived tur-bulence of that magnitude. The flexibility of the ParaPlane's wing was, in our humble opinion, a major factor in our survival.

Gene and I talked about that unbelievable flight all the way home. Even today, when I think about it, it still sends shivers down my spine. No other "fright flight" that I've encountered can even come close to equalling the "terror factor" of this one, but there are a few other incidents in my log book that are worth men-tioning. Now, bear in mind that most of my flights have been ex-tremely enjoyable, and I'm really nit-picking when I explain the difficult ones. However, few though they be, these flights are really very important in understanding the capabilities of a powered parachute type ultralight aircraft.

It was July 19th, 1986. Forty eight excellent flights had passed since the cow field incident, and they had steadily built my confidence. It was a gray, overcast Saturday, and I had decided to visit a rod and gun club that a friend of mine named Dan Harple had invited me to, for my 88th flight. Dan had assured me that there was plenty of room on their field for me to take off, according to the minimum distance that I told him was necessary. When I arrived, it was apparent that he was correct in his estimation of the amount of field area. There was only one small problem. The field was surrounded by forty foot tall trees.

At first, I thought that there was no way I could fly off this field, but for the heck of it, I walked the length of it to check it out. There was no wind to speak of, which would only increase the distance required. Quite a number of people from the club began milling around, asking me questions about the "unusual aircraft". They seemed disappointed when I told them that after checking it out, I didn't think I could use the field. I don't know whether it was peer pressure or just pride on my part, but after a considerable amount of thought, I decided that there might be a way I could pull it off. At least, I felt, it was worth a try.

If I were to begin as far back on the field as possible and get the chute into "flight ready" mode before reaching a critical point on the field, I just might be able to clear the tree tops. Sure, it was risky, but all I had to do was abort the takeoff if I passed what I determined to be the critical point on the field. My mind was made up. I would at least give it a try.

The weather was deteriorating. A storm front was coming in, and rain was predicted for late in the afternoon. Still, there was no wind at ground level.

Standing on the far edge of the field, I made a rough calculation as to the climb angle I would need to clear the tree line with a half tank of gas, eighty degree temperature and no wind. Fixing my eyes on a clump of grass in the field, I walked over and pushed a small stick into the ground. This would be my critical liftoff point. If my calculations proved out correct, rolling any further than this without lifting off would not allow me to clear the tree line.

After recruiting a couple of wing holders and briefing them, I set the ParaPlane up as close to the south tree line as possible. I was really nervous. There were doubts in my mind. I prayed that I would have the sense to abort the takeoff if necessary. Once the adrenalin starts to flow, my normal tendency is to go for it. I was not known for aborting takeoffs.

The surface winds were calm, but from my seat in the cart, I could see the tops of the trees swaying on the north end of the field. This should have tipped me off that there would be downdrafts to contend with. But in my psyched up nervous state of mind, it didn't register as a problem.

The short engine warm up period was over, so I signaled my inexperienced wing holders to let go of the chute. Perhaps I added too much throttle, in hopes of achieving a quick kite up, or perhaps one wing holder held on too long, but only half of the chute opened, yanking the cart sideways. Immediately, I corrected my course and continued the takeoff run. The critical marker was coming up fast. Finally, the chute took its proper shape, and I lifted off about five feet short of the marker. My climb to the tree tops had begun. There was no way I could abort now. If I did, I would run smack into the tree line. And there was no room to turn around. The field wasn't wide enough for that maneuver.

The engines sounded strong, and initially the ParaPlane climbed as I had anticipated it would. But as I got to within forty feet of the tree line, the ParaPlane leveled off. It was not climbing as it should have. Then it dawned on me. I was encountering mechanical turbulence from wind blowing over the tree line. Frantically, I dropped my legs down and held the throttle hard against the stop in hopes of getting every inch of climb rate possible. At this point, things didn't look good.

As I neared the tree line with seconds to spare, I felt the cart lift as if by divine intervention. With my legs dangling, I winced uncontrollably and shut my eyes tight. It appeared the trees and I were about to get better acquainted.

Although I could not look, I know I hit the tops of the trees because the upper branches slashed into my dangling legs. When the slashing ceased, I opened my eyes to see the trees fading away beneath me. I had made it! The feeling of relief was overwhelming.

For ten minutes, I circled the field mostly to regain my composure. Then I executed a perfect three point short landing on the south end of the inadequate field. Everyone on the ground was impressed with my performance. They asked me to return and I politely declined. Once was more than enough for this field. These people probably didn't realize it, but I was very lucky to have pulled this flight off without a major mishap. It was a close call. Much too close. There was no room for error, and error had occurred. I vowed that I would never attempt another flight if there was any doubt in my mind whatsoever.

Only four flights after this one, on my ninety second flight, I encountered my first (and hopefully last) emergency landing due to equipment failure. It was August fourth, on a gorgeous Monday afternoon after work. The temperature was a balmy eighty degrees, and the wind was light out of the west. As I often did when I had no one to help, I went to the airport alone and set everything up by myself. The serenity of the airfield when I'm unaccompanied often puts me into a peaceful reflective mood. As I aimed the ParaPlane down the grass alongside the cross runway to the west, I couldn't help but notice the beginning of a gorgeous sunset.

My plan was to fly for about half an hour, crossing the Taunton River into Somerset, so I could watch the sun go down during the course of the flight. My pre-flight procedure went routinely, and during the warm up period, the engines sounded good. My takeoff was excellent, with the chute forming quickly and a short ground roll. Within a few minutes, I reached three hundred and fifty feet, leveled off and headed for the river. Everything was going smoothly, and I felt very relaxed. Normally, I never cross the river unless I have at least eight hundred feet of altitude. This time, for some unknown reason, I simply decided to remain at three hundred and fifty feet.

The setting sun was a bright orange orb, on the verge of kissing the horizon, as I neared the center of the river. Vivid red reflections danced across the hundreds of window panes that dotted the landscape ahead of me. The spectacle was awesome and eerily hypnotic -- until a clanging noise broke the spell.

It was a strange sound, not unlike an automobile engine pinging. In an attempt to locate the source, I turned around as far as my neck muscles would allow, expecting to see something hanging loose on one of the engines. Everything appeared to be intact, but the noise persisted. It did not seem rhythmic, nor very loud. The ParaPlane was still flying normally, so I decided not to worry about it.

What I failed to realize, is that I was wearing earplugs. The noise had to be very loud, in order for me to have heard it over the exhaust noise. Thinking all was well, I continued on my odyssey. But I could not stop wondering what that strange noise was. Well, it didn't take long for me to find out.

About thirty seconds after the noise began, the engine exhaust drone started to waver high and low in pitch. I turned my head around just in time to watch one of the propellors come to an abrupt halt! My immediate reaction was to push the throttle wide open. The remaining engine sped up to maximum and sounded strong. Simultaneously, I checked my position. I had just passed the middle of the river. There was no way I could return to the airport, but for some reason, I wasn't really worried. At my present rate of descent I knew I could make it to the Somerset shoreline.

Pierce's Beach was directly in front of me, and next to it was a baseball field. I set my sights on a strip of grass alongside the ball field. When I neared the shoreline, my altitude was down to seventy feet. I could have landed on the beach, but it wasn't too smooth, and I felt that the loose sand could tip the cart over.

There was no time to turn around and land into the wind. My altitude was now too low, I would have to land with the wind. As I approached the grass strip, I throttled back, and at about ten feet from touchdown, I went to full throttle. The ParaPlane made a perfect gentle landing! The only difficulty I encountered was the chute blowing over my head and landing in front of me. But it was no big deal. Actually, I thoroughly enjoyed the whole scenario! It was an exciting challenge to have to make an emergency landing under acceptable wind conditions. I had gone over all kinds of power failure situations in my head, and finally, I was able to act one out. It felt terrific to have met the challenge triumphantly.

As soon as I touched down, I was surrounded by curious onlookers. Before I could pack the chute, a police car pulled alongside of me.

"What are you doing here?" he inquired.

"I don't want to be here," I said. "An engine quit over the river and I had to make an emergency landing."

"What is that thing?" he asked.

"A ParaPlane!" I said proudly.

"Have you got a license to fly that thing?"

"You don't need a license, per se, but I do have a certificate showing that I'm a competent pilot. I assure you officer, I know what I'm doing. I've got almost one hundred flights in this thing. This is the first time I ever lost an engine."

The officer scanned my first flight certificate quickly, nodded his head, then asked me how I was going to get the thing out of there.

"Well, if it starts, I'll fly it out of here."

"Have you got enough room?"

"No problem," I assured.

Actually, I would have loved to fly it out of the park, but no matter how hard I tried, the left engine would not fire. In frustration, I pulled so hard on the starter cord, I yanked it right out of the engine. Now, my trailer was the only option.

I didn't know it at the time, but the engine had burned a piston due to a lean fuel mixture. It would never have started because the compression was too low.

"What are you going to do now?" the cop asked.

"If I can get a ride to the airport, I'll pick up my trailer, and be back here in twenty minutes."

"I'll give you a ride!" was the mass response from the crowd of onlookers.

"Great!" I said, as I picked the closest person.

The cop agreed to watch my ParaPlane, and I left and returned in short order with my car. Bystanders helped me to load the ParaPlane on the trailer. I thanked the officer for waiting, waved goodbye to the crowd, and arrived home at about the same time as I would have under normal circumstance.

It turned out to be quite an experience, and not really a true "fright flight", but it sure had the potential to be one, so I felt it was necessary to include it.

Only the three flights previously described, and of course my first and second flights, which I covered in detail earlier, qualified as "fright flights" out of my first one hundred and seventy Para-Plane adventures. During my next hundred excursions, six other incidents occurred that brought about strong feelings of anxiety.

Flight number 172, proved to be a bit unnerving. It was on a warm Wednesday on the first of July, in 1987, and I had the day off from work. I asked Pip to meet me at Myricks, where I decided to fly a cross country to Fall River Airport. Although I normally fly only in the early morning and late afternoon, this time it was twelve noon when I became airborne. There were a few clouds around, and thunderstorms were predicted for late afternoon.

About halfway into the flight, at about six hundred feet, I flew into a gray area of sky and felt a little turbulence. Suddenly, air began to rush up from under me, billowing out my pants. There was a sinking feeling similar to what you experience when an elevator begins to accelerate upward. A quick glance at the altimeter showed a rapid increase in altitude. My ParaPlane, it seemed, was caught in the initial stages of a thunderstorm forming!

Trying not to panic, I brought the throttle to idle, in hopes of halting the ascent, but the ParaPlane kept on climbing! I had gone from six hundred to twelve hundred feet in seconds! If I were a glider pilot, I probably would have been thrilled to have found such a strong thermal, but I wanted to go **down**, not up!

I tried a full deflection spiral, to reduce my altitude, but the climb continued. Finally, at about sixteen hundred feet, there was another short bout of turbulence, and the ParaPlane began to descend, ever so slowly. I started to breathe again. What a feeling of relief! My mind was beginning to create illusions of being sucked into the stratosphere. I wanted no part of that. When my altitude reached one hundred feet, I leveled off and flew the rest of the way to the airport just above the trees. It was a hard way to learn why most people don't fly ultralights in the middle of the day. Especially when it's hot and humid.

Flight number 177, was another classic. It was my longest cross country to date. On July 15th, in the early evening, I arranged to meet a friend, named Dave Humphrey, at the airport. He agreed to drive my car to a field in Rochester, Mass., about thirty five miles away. Dave is a very competent pilot in his own right, who has ably performed aerobatics, and has quite a few flight hours logged in conventional aircraft. We spent a lot of time shooting the breeze about our mutual interests.

By the time I got my act together and began the flight, it was almost sundown. There was a light west tailwind, that I figured would allow me to reach the field before dark. Halfway into the flight, however, the tailwind turned into a headwind and slowed me down considerably. At the point in time when I should have been on the ground, I still had miles to go.

Before long, it became difficult to see. As the darkness increased, I turned on a pocket emergency strobe light that I decided to bring along at the last minute. It didn't help me to see, but at least it made me visible to others.

I began to lose my bearings. Landmarks that I had been relying on were becoming obscure. Suddenly, I had no idea where I was. It was just too dark. If my heading was correct, I should have been close to the field, but all I could discern were gray, distant city lights. Directly in front of me, total darkness had completely erased the landscape. I had to rely on the flashing strobe light to read my altimeter.

All of a sudden, the glow of a car's headlights appeared about a quarter of a mile away. They faintly illuminated what seemed to be an open field. When I reached the area, I lowered my altitude and tried to identify the shadowy figure that was standing in front of the high beams. It was my friend Dave! He had driven my car out onto the field to help guide me. My sense of impending doom instantly turned to feelings of elation.

The headlights from the car, radiating through the grass, and dimly outlining a section of field, were all I had to land by. I prepared to touch down on what appeared to be the surface of the field. In actuality, it was the top of the grass, which had grown three feet tall since I last visited the field. Upon contact with the top surface of the dense grass, the ParaPlane fell three feet and came to a very abrupt halt. If I hadn't had a seat belt on, I'd have been cast into the weeds.

Apart from being startled by the landing, and picking grass out of my shoes and the airframe for two days after, the flight ended on a successful note. Of course, without Dave's assistance and quick thinking, things might not have turned out so well. If I learned anything from that flight, it was "never embark on a cross country flight when darkness is imminent."

On my 190th flight, I was on my way to work, flying from Fall River, Massachusetts, to Portsmouth, Rhode Island. This was a once a year ritual for me, and a twenty mile flight. Usually, I would land in a nearby ballfield. On this day, the twelfth of August, something strange occurred when I was about half a mile from my intended destination.

While relaxing in my little "sky chair" at seven hundred feet, I was shaken by a tremendously loud clang type noise. Scanning the airframe, I couldn't perceive anything wrong, so I dismissed it and continued on. Shortly thereafter, as I was preparing to land, I heard the noise again, followed immediately by a second, even louder noise. The ParaPlane was still flying well, so even though I was concerned about the source of the noise, I proceeded to execute a flawless landing.

After packing the chute, I was lifting it over the cart when I saw something that made my jaw drop. Both of the wooden propellors were shattered! The tips were splintered beyond repair. Something had hit them while I was flying, but I was unable to find anything missing from the aircraft. This led me to theorize that perhaps someone had shot at me! However, after a careful examination of the power system, I found three belt adjustment shims missing from the engine mounting bolts. Three shims, three loud bangs--it made sense. It was quite a relief to know that no one was using me for target practice.

A while back, I was supposed to have the engine mounting bolts updated to a larger size by the factory. Well, I never got around to it. Now, it seemed I would have to pay the price for my procrastination. It was a fortunate thing for me that I was not hurt in any way by the flying pieces of shims and props.

Complications on this next "fright flight" were due to weather conditions that "seemed" to be perfect. Flight 211 began as the smoothest excursion that I had ever been on. It occurred on November 15th, 1987, on a dead calm Sunday afternoon. The temperature was thirty seven degrees. I was returning from a pleasant tour of the city water supply area. The pond water reflected the trees on the shoreline like a mirror. The air could not have been calmer. From the beginning, the flight was super smooth, and I flew until my fuel tank was almost empty, not wanting to waste a second of a seemingly ideal flying day.

On my way back, as I flew over the huge landfill next to the airport, I was startled by a short period of "moderate" turbulence. Immediately, I grabbed for something to hold on to. It only lasted a few short seconds, and I attributed it to heated air rising from the compost of the dump.

Just north of the landfill, at 800 feet, I began my descent for landing. At about 500 feet, I sensed something that felt weird. It was a strange falling sensation. A quick glance at my altimeter confirmed that I was indeed dropping in altitude at a rapid pace. Instinctively, I pushed the throttle to the limit, in hopes of climbing. The engines sounded strong, but the rapid descent continued. Looking up, I could see the chute was toward the rear, indicating a climbing mode, but the craft was still falling at a rate of over 400 feet a minute. There didn't appear to be anything mechanically wrong. At full throttle, I should have been climbing, not falling. It didn't make any sense, and it had me scared. The ground was coming up fast, and I wanted to do something to negate the plunge, but all I could do was wait.

The ParaPlane dropped from 500 feet to 100 feet in less than a minute, at full throttle! It seemed that an undesired landing was imminent, and I began to brace myself for impact. Then, at about 80 feet, the ParaPlane started to level off. I continued to hold the throttle at maximum, and after a few seconds the craft started to climb, as it should have. At that point, I headed straight for a landing spot near my car. Oddly, as I approached the landing area, the air was as calm as it had been earlier. I was able to touch down very gently, and precisely where I wanted to.

This type of unwanted descent has never happened to me before or since flight 211. The only logical reason for it that I could come up with was that the strong downdraft was probably created by heat rising from the dump in the super calm air. Apparently, as I neared the ground, the column of falling air disbursed, allowing me to break free. If it ever happens again, I'll know what to expect, and I won't be as nervous.

The mishap that occurred on flight 219, January 24th, 1988, was not due to the weather or to equipment failure. It was a self-inflicted mishap.

My intention on this flight, was to have my cousin Pip take some unique photos of me flying in various precarious positions. After doing a number of full deflection turns at low altitudes, I decided that flying through the top branches of a tree would look spectacular on film. I assumed that the craft would easily float through the soft, thin, spindly upper limbs. Well, you know what happens when you "assume".

When I hit those "soft" branches, they felt more like hardened steel. They swung the ParaPlane cart rapidly from side to side. Then a stiff branch caught hold of a support cable, twisting the cart sideways.

Held back by the branch, the cart started to plummet from the top of the thirty five foot tall tree. In desperation, I slipped my arm out from under the shoulder harness, reached out as far as I could, and tore the branch loose from the cable. Instantly, the cart dropped out of the tree and fell until the slack came out of the lines going to the chute. There was just enough time to level off before contacting the ground, allowing for a normal landing only a few yards from the tree line.

My pulse was racing as I exited the cart, and asked Pip how he thought **that** photo was going to look.

"Well", he said, "I was so excited when you caught the tree branches, I forgot to take the picture!"

I couldn't believe it. There's no question it was stupid for me to voluntarily hit a tree, but it would have been nice to at least have a photo of it!

The last in my selection of "traumatic treks" occurred on a warm Saturday evening, August 20th, 1988. Flight 244 didn't seem so bad at the time, but the more I think about it, the more it scares me. Of all my flights to date, it is the one that had the greatest potential for disaster.

A fellow named John Belmarce, had purchased a Para-Plane from me. It was one of three that I had acquired from a defunct Canadian dealer, in hopes of starting my own dealership. I couldn't locate any land to lease for training, so I opted to sell them.

John is from New Bedford, Mass., a sister city of Fall River. He passed his first flight course, which I had arranged for him through a New Hampshire dealer, with flying colors. Shortly thereafter, I took him to the airport in Fall River for his first flight in his own ParaPlane. The flight went exceptionally well.

On the following day, we brought both of our ParaPlanes to the airport. John was full of enthusiasm and wonder, and he reminded me of myself on my early flights, except he didn't seem to be as nervous as I had been. This was to be his third flight, and the first time we would both be in the air together. Since he was just a rookie, I thoroughly briefed him on the rules of the airport, especially that he keep a sharp eye out for small planes.

John took off first, so that I could observe and signal him if he were to encounter any difficulties. His launch was flawless, and I hurriedly followed him into the air. We discussed our flight plans before taking off, but there was one thing that I neglected to mention, probably because I didn't think that it was necessary.

As we flew side by side, he began to fly too close to me. We were still about one hundred feet apart, but I didn't want to chance a collision, so I kept turning left and away from him.

He obviously didn't realize why I was turning and waving him away, because he turned every time I did, and kept getting closer. I was so busy keeping an eye on him, I didn't realize that I had ventured into the landing approach zone utilized by conventional aircraft.

We were flying at 800 feet. I was looking over at him, instead of watching what was ahead of me. I turned my head forward just in time to see a single engine light plane, directly in front of me! He was not fifty feet away, and closing fast! Instantly, I kicked my right steering arm as hard as I could, and as far as I could. Simultaneously, I chopped the throttle back to idle. The pilot of the light plane must have seen me at the same instant that I noticed him, because he banked hard to his right and pulled up sharply. I could see the underbelly of his plane clearly, as he flashed overhead within a few feet of me. Although I never found out who the pilot was, I could see his face well enough to tell it was a man. Some time later, I was told that a pilot had filed a report revealing a near miss with an ultralight aircraft on that day.

It was a very close call. If we had not both taken split second evasive action, I probably would not have been able to write this story.

The incident was not John's fault. It was my fault. I should have explained things better.

What I should have done when I felt there was a problem, was return to the field and land, so that I could explain to him my reasons for maintaining a safe distance between us. It was a lesson hard learned, as were all of the "fright flight" scenarios. It is my sincere hope that I have learned enough now, to avoid having to write a sequel to this chapter. Also, if these incidents help just one person from making the same mistakes, then it will have been well worth my efforts to explain them.

Every flight I have taken, whether it be fun or frightening has had some aspect of awe and beauty associated with it. Flying a powered parachute opens up a whole new world, a whole new dimension. It is, in fact, exotic. The world you see every day from the ground, expands into a bold new realm when viewed from the unconstrained seat of a ParaPlane. In my humble opinion, there isn't a more economical, safer way to take to the skies, and the emphasis is definitely on safety. In the next chapter, I believe I can prove my point.

CHAPTER 9

SUPER SAFE FLYING

For those of you out there who think any form of flying can be dangerous, you won't get an argument from me. You're "dead" right! However, while it is true that flying can be a perilous activity, the same can be said for walking across the street. Any activity that you plunge into without proper thought can result in disaster. The key to succeeding at any endeavor is to know the facts. Flying a powered parachute can be a very safe and rewarding recreational activity, if you learn the basics and know your limitations.

In this chapter, I shall attempt to prove beyond a shadow of a doubt that <u>you</u> <u>can</u> venture aloft safely. Veteran pilots can skip this chapter if they so desire, but be advised, included are some interesting anecdotes of strange encounters.

The first and most important aspect of flying is not the takeoff. It is unquestionably the pre-flight procedure. A proper and thorough pre-flight procedure is absolutely imperative to insure a safe flight. Once you have committed the pre-flight procedure to memory, it doesn't take long to perform it. And if you have a pet peeve about something that isn't included in the pre-flight, by all means include it! You should add to the procedure any check that will make you feel more comfortable and secure.

Next in line is the takeoff. This is probably the area that most ParaPlane pilots have trouble with. If on your takeoff roll, you stray too far off the wind line, or the parachute is not fully inflated, the cart can tip over if you apply enough throttle for lift. A rollover is generally due to pilot error, and can be easily avoided with the proper training. Although a smart person wouldn't be attempting a flight in adverse wind conditions, it's also possible that the wind could shift enough during a takeoff roll and cause a tipover.

Assuming the worst happens and you do roll the cart over, there is really nothing to fear. You are safely strapped in by a lap belt and shoulder harness, and you are well protected by the airframe. I have witnessed many a rollover, and have yet to see anyone seriously hurt. The cart usually pole vaults around on the arms and framework, with the surprised pilot along for the ride. Some flips have occurred while at full throttle (you should at least kill the engines) having rolled violently, but each time the pilot emerged with, at most, superficial cuts and bruises. It was obvious that their pride was hurt more than anything else.

Here are two important rules to remember.

Rule No. 1: Never add enough throttle to cause the cart to lift off the ground, unless your chute is fully opened and centered over the cart.

On a "no wind" day, not enough throttle, and you won't get the chute up--too much throttle before the chute is formed properly, and you could tip the cart over. You have to find that happy medium, and it's easy. If you feel the cart start to lift, and you know the chute is not ready, bring the throttle back just a little bit. After a few tries, you will know how much throttle is needed, and how much is too much.

Beginning chute inflation.

Chute ready for liftoff.

Rule No. 2: If you are not comfortable with the takeoff, for instance, if the wind seems erratic or the chute won't fully open (you could have a tangled chute line), by all means, abort the takeoff!

If you are prudent, and follow rules one and two religiously, you should <u>never</u> encounter a rollover. Personally, in over 425 takeoffs, I have only rolled the cart over once, and that was before I knew about rule number one! Also, I have only had to abort two takeoffs. So you see, you can launch a ParaPlane properly, even on your first flight, if you listen to your instructor, and follow the rules.

Sometimes when the chute is opened and centered, and you apply full throttle for takeoff, the cart will lift off crooked, perhaps from a gust of wind. Under these circumstances, you should continue on with the launch. The cart will stabilize itself as soon as it leaves the ground. If you do abort, you will almost surely tip over. Except for this situation, you should never be embarrassed to abort a takeoff. It's a simple procedure to relaunch, and it's a damn sight better than destroying some of your equipment, and having to put your flying on hold until you receive replacement parts.

Most of the problems people encounter happen on the ground during launch. Once your powered parachute is airborne, there is not much to be concerned about. A ParaPlane with its throttle set for level flight will fly straight and level until such time as you initiate a turn, or change the throttle setting to climb or descend. It would fly just as well with 150 pounds of ballast on board, as with a pilot. Your hands and feet are free of duty, allowing you to relax, take pictures, or whatever. Well...I wouldn't recommend falling asleep, there <u>are</u> other aircraft to look out for.

Another unique safety factor associated with a ParaPlane is the fact that you have a fully operational recovery system working for you at all times. You're hanging under a parachute! In the extremely unlikely event that you should pass out in the thing, the craft will eventually land all by itself, and let you down easy. Try <u>that</u> in a conventional airplane! Of course, who knows where you would end up, but at least you would have an excellent chance of survival.

Here's another special safety consideration. A ParaPlane cannot dive. If you should screw up in a fixed wing aircraft, you could conceivably dive into the ground at a potentially fatal high rate of speed. This is not possible with a powered parachute. Engine running or not, the craft will only descend slowly, at about seven miles per hour. Even without power, you can still steer, and you still have forward airspeed, about twenty one miles per hour. Also the craft is virtually stall proof. And with such a small cart and a flexible wing, you can land almost anywhere. Flight wise, what could be safer?

Okay. Your launch can be done safely, and flying can be done safely, so what about the landing? I'm glad you asked. Bringing a ParaPlane in for a landing is a piece of cake, as long as you head into the wind. If you like, you can aim the aircraft for the spot you wish to land on, and--don't just do something-- sit there! The ParaPlane will virtually land all by itself. All you have to do is shut down the engines on touchdown. The only rule here is, if you want to level off to soften the landing, add throttle a few feet before you want to level off. The cart takes a second or two to swing forward and change the wing's angle of attack. During this short period, you will continue to accelerate at the same drop angle. Therefore, if you are too close to the ground, and you add throttle, you will only hit harder. After a few low passes, you will know at what altitude to throttle up for a smooth touchdown. That's all there is to it.

Now, don't get me wrong. You shouldn't just read this book, then go on out and fly your friend's ParaPlane without any train- ing. That would be foolish. A few hours training with a certified instructor, is all that's required, and you will be a para-pilot the same day, even if you've never flown anything before. The tips that I'm giving you in this book should save you a lot of potential grief, and make you a better pilot in much less time.

What? You're still not assured that it's safe? Fine. Here are a few factual "pilot errors" that have occurred over the years. I won't mention any names to save them the embarrassment. If these featherbrained scenarios fail to convince you of the safety of this activity, I don't know what will. Maybe nothing.

After a perfectly normal takeoff, I was circling around waiting for another Para-pilot to launch. He decided to use a longer area of grass to take off, even though he was way off the wind line. With his chute half folded, and way over on the left side of the cart, he added full throttle. I don't know why. The cart accelerated rapidly, then flipped over so fast that, if you blinked your eyes, you would have missed it. The top of the airframe hit the ground so violently, it dug a three foot long furrow, six inches deep in the hard packed grass. The embarrassed pilot emerged with nothing but a sore shoulder.

Another fellow performed a normal takeoff on an early flight. Then for some foolish reason, before he gained any altitude, he turned sharply, and flew right into a row of electric power lines! The rear landing gear hooked onto one of the wires, and the would-be pilot dangled upside down for over an hour, with gas dripping and sparks flying. When the power company finally lowered him down, the airframe was burned full of holes from shorting across the high tension lines. Amazingly, there was no fire, and he was completely unhurt. I'd venture a guess, though, that when it was over, he had to at least change his underwear.

This next one is another classic. A para-pilot with only a few flights logged, decided to use a high school parking lot to fly out of. With the cart on the wind line, and headed straight for the school building, he lifted off fine, but failed to consider the effect of the wind coming over the roof of the building and causing mechanical turbulence. Consequently, the poor fellow didn't get enough altitude, and flew smack into the brick wall of the gymnasium! The front of the cart folded like an accordion, and the twisted airframe, with the baffled pilot on board, slid down the wall to the ground on the chute. The fool walked away from an accident that would surely have buried him, had he been in a conventional aircraft. All of these people were fortunate enough to have been flying the very forgiving ParaPlane.

I'm sure there are more lame-brained incidents that have occurred out there, but I am unaware of them. The ParaPlane has been on the scene now for over six years, and to my knowledge, not one single fatality can be attributed to a failure of any part of the craft.

There is one incident that I know of where an elderly man had a heart attack while flying on his first flight. It was said that he had a history of heart disease. Apparently he lost consciousness, and was unable to maintain control. The ParaPlane let him down easy, but unfortunately, he landed in a river. In my opinion, this fatality was not the fault of the aircraft.

Since the invention of the ParaPlane in 1983, many thousands of people have flown. Most of them taking to the air for the first time, and all of them soloing on their first flight, without any serious consequences. With proper training, there's no reason to believe that this trend will not continue. If you are looking for a safe and secure way to fly, look no further.

When it comes to "super safe flying", a powered parachute has no equal. If your car breaks down, you can pull over to the side of the road. In an airplane, you don't have that option. In a ParaPlane, however, you can drop safely into many places, making it almost as easy as parking a car, unless you are flying over a forest where there is no clear place to land. In that case, wouldn't you rather be on a parachute going slow than in an airplane going fast?

The ParaPlane Corporation has clearly designed the craft with safety in mind. Only the very finest aircraft quality components are used. Support cables, for instance, which have to carry about 80 pounds of weight each, were pull tested to over 4000 pounds, with no breakage occurring. The chute or wing is made of "ripstop" nylon. Should you tear it by snagging it on something, the stitch is locked, and the rip will not continue. I have flown with small rips in the fabric, with no adverse effects.

Personally, I have great faith in the structural integrity of the ParaPlane. My severe turbulence episode in New York State, proved to me that the entire unit can withstand far more stress than it should ever normally encounter. If properly maintained, there is no reason to worry about structural failure.

Flying out in the open used to scare the living daylights out of me. But, again, there is no reason to worry. The seat belt is integrated with a shoulder harness. Even if you were to release the belt, you would have to slip your arms under both straps of the shoulder harness before you could exit the vehicle.

Still, it took some getting used to, being so out in the open, so high in the air. But believe me, it has been well worth the effort it took to condition myself to feel secure. The door is now open for me to enjoy many more recreational flights of fancy. The possibilities are limitless. In the next chapter, I will explore some imaginative prospects that I have dreamed up for future flights.

One final note: I have learned to love wearing a seat belt. In a ParaPlane, it gives you a safe and secure feeling, and, it's a must! Ironically, that secure feeling has carried over to when I'm driving my car. Before my flying experiences, I never wore a seat belt in my car. It was just too much of a bother. Now I really appreciate it, and wear it all the time. It's a great feeling! Flying a ParaPlane has made driving my car; less risky. How's that for safety?

CHAPTER 10

BECKONING SKIES

Before the advent of the ultralight aircraft, the average person who wanted to fly, usually only dreamt about venturing aloft. Cost was the major prohibiting factor. When the ultralight came on the scene a few years back, things began to look promising. Powered hang gliders and wire braced fixed wings, offered basic "no license" flight capabilities at a relatively low cost.

As time went on, these aircraft became quite popular, but soon they developed a reputation as a very dangerous recreational flight activity. Fatalities occurred, and they were magnified by the media, which all but destroyed the ultralight industry. Only the heartiest of souls flew these early ultralights, and I was not one of them.

Through the years, major improvements have been incorporated into the design safety of these aircraft, making them far less risky an undertaking, as they were in their infancy. They are making a gradual comeback, slowed considerably by all the bad press surrounding them.

The ParaPlane entered the picture in the middle of this safety controversy. Because it falls into the same classification as an ultralight craft, it has been unjustly looked upon as a perilous activity, in some people's eyes. The basic principles of powered parachute flight differ considerably from conventional fixed wing aircraft, as I have previously explained.

Powered parachutes, should have earned a strong reputation as the safest, simplest, most economical way to fly recreationally. The only reason they may not have, is that not enough people are familiar with them. Very few people are aware of the tremendous safety characteristics of these aircraft. It is my sincere hope that this book will better inform the world of a truly marvelous and safe way to fly for the sheer fun and immense satisfaction of it.

In the last few years, another powered parachute called the "Buckeye" was introduced. Although the principle is the same, there are a few differences between the Buckeye and the Para-Plane. The Buckeye uses only one engine, and has had the trim of the chute altered to compensate for torque effect. They are sold in kit form. Some of my friends are owners of Buckeyes and they swear by them. The Buckeye appears to be well designed, and utilizes separate steering for ground handling. The seating position is more reclined, and the version I saw was equipped with only a lap belt. A four point harness would offer more security.

Recently, a close cousin of the Buckeye, called the "Parascender" has arrived on the scene. This model sports larger "rough terrain" type tires, and a heavily padded "arm chair" style seat. Both models utilize a fiberglass spring arm axle, as opposed to the square aluminum tubing used to suspend the Para-Plane. Prices vary with all units, depending upon accessories, but similarly equipped models cost virtually the same.

For my money, I prefer the backup capabilities of the two engines on the ParaPlane. The power system is a little more complex, but in my experience, and with proper care, I have had very few engine problems. It's extremely unlikely that you will lose both engines at the same time, unless you run out of gas.

The Buckeye and Parascender utilize the popular Rotax engine. The ParaPlane uses two Solo engines. All models fly at the same slow airspeed. The best way to choose one, in my opinion, would be to fly them all, then select the aircraft you are most comfortable with.

Many exciting things are now happening in the world of powered parachutes. All three companies are currently offering a high performance canopy option. I have flown ParaPlane's new chute, and let me tell you, this chute really performs! At my weight of 130 lbs., the climb rate must have been over 1000 ft. per minute, and at a temperature of ninety degrees! With power set at idle, I landed as softly as I would have at half throttle with my old seven cell chute. I believe with this chute, I could fly level with only one engine running.

The fabric on my original six year old chute is as good as the day I purchased it, so I cannot justify buying a new one. This durability factor is another reason why the cost of ownership is so low.

Powered parachute clubs are now forming in different parts of the country. There is an informal gathering of ParaPlane pilots in New Hampshire, and a Buckeye group in New York. A friendly rivalry has developed between the Buckeyes and the ParaPlanes that makes our get togethers really interesting.

Good natured insults fly back and forth between the two groups regarding the flying abilities of pilots, and the differences between machines. I look forward to these events because there's never a dull moment, and everyone has a whole lot of fun. Through these meets, I have met some of the nicest people, and the unique friendships that have developed are second to none.

Without question, there have been many exciting flying moments over the past six years. On New Years Day, 1987, I tried flying off snow for the first time. While many people were nursing their hangovers, I went to the airport early in the morning to try out a set of homemade skis! They were fashioned from two sets of plastic children's skis. The front ski had to turn, so I mounted it on the fork. On the rear, I clamped the skis on the wheels, which I tied so they couldn't turn. Then I added bungie cords to the front of each ski, so the rear of the ski would contact first on landing. It was a makeshift setup, but I felt it would be safe and effective.

First flight with skis.

In the air, the ParaPlane flew as well as it did with wheels, but the view was something else! The aerial panorama I was normally familiar with, looked like a whole new area. The thin carpet of snow had obscured many of the landmarks I was accustomed to seeing. Everything was white, and it was beautiful. Fields, farms, and backyards glistened brightly, reflecting the sunlight with great intensity. Without sunglasses, I would have been snow blind.

Snow flying can increase your potential landing areas, because the snow smooths out sections of land that would otherwise be unlandable.

On February 28th, 1987, I flew off of a frozen pond for the first time. The ice was over a foot thick. There were tire tracks on the surface, so I figured if the ice could support a car, I should have no problem. It was quite windy, so I recruited Pip and Danny to hold onto the chute. We pushed the ParaPlane out onto the South Watuppa Pond in Fall River. My available takeoff room was almost unlimited.

In the air, there was never an instant when I couldn't have landed safely. It was possible to fly for miles, and still have the pond under me in case of emergency. The vast expanse of ice conjured up visions of what it might be like flying over the North Pole or Antarctica. In the middle of the pond, from about nine hundred feet up, my ground crew looked like members of an Arctic expedition stranded on the frozen tundra. They were dwarfed by a seemingly endless and barren world of white. Ironically, this alien looking region was only a few miles from home.

Although I have accomplished a great deal of things with my ParaPlane, I feel there are many more challenges left to explore. Cross country flights of great lengths would be fun to embark on. Some day I would like to try a trans-continental flight, from the Pacific to the Atlantic Ocean. This would require a full ground crew following, but I believe it would be possible, and a fascinating challenge.

Pin point landings into tiny areas are also an inviting possibility. I look forward to the day when powered parachutes will be a welcome addition to carnivals and city park festivities. On my 200th flight, I ventured into this arena by landing in my tiny backyard!

Before I tried this "stunt", I worked out all the logistics, and was sure in my mind that I could do it. My preparation paid off, and the actual landing was much easier than I had anticipated. With a powered parachute, many such landings are quite feasible. The possibilities are endless.

Short takeoffs are also attainable, under the proper conditions. This area leaves more room for error, but I have no doubt that many a park or field can be utilized safely. With a steady ten m.p.h. wind, I have lifted off in as little as twenty feet from a standing start. You can travel up to cruising altitude in less forward distance with a headwind, because your climb angle is steeper.

For anyone who wants to fly a powered parachute often, the ideal situation is to have your own land to fly from. You could fly anytime that the conditions warranted it, if you owned a farm, or had a good sized backyard with no obstructions. This would allow one the freedom of taking to the sky at a moments notice, rather than driving to a field that was miles away.

One of my unrealized dreams is to fly down into the Grand Canyon on a ParaPlane. It would be fun to get together with another para-pilot, or two, fly down into the canyon, stay overnight in sleeping bags next to the Colorado River, then return the following day. The flight down would require very little fuel, leaving you with an almost full tank to fly back to the top of the gorge with. Personally, I can't think of a more enjoyable way to view the Grand Canyon.

Another fuel conserving way to "sail the sky," would be to take off near a mountain with an updraft. Once airborne, you could ride the rising currents of air for a good long time, perhaps even killing the engines and floating in silence, if the updrafts were strong enough.

There are majestic mountains and winding rivers all over this country, just begging to be explored by air; painted canyons and deep chasms waiting to be visited; rugged badland areas accessible only from above. There are deep woodlands with thick underbrush where few people have ventured. Nature has provided us with many rare landscapes heretofore unvisited by the average person. The ParaPlane opens the door to scenic wonders of epic proportions. I know. I've been there.

If you decide to embark on a cross country trip by car or recreational vehicle, a ParaPlane would be a fantastic fun machine to have stashed in your trunk. As of this writing, powered parachutes are not a common sight in most areas, but I see a day on the horizon when they will be standard fare on many vacations. This is an activity that entire families can safely take part in, with proper training. Only the very young, and people who weight over two hundred and fifty pounds would be excluded from enjoying personal flight.

Acrophobic individuals should take note. My own successful confrontation with my fear of height, shows that it is entirely possible to overcome a phobia, if your desire to prevail is strong enough. Flying was something I always thought would have to remain a dream for me. With a little perseverance, I turned my idle apparitions into true flights of fancy. Now I can live the life I once only imagined. After all, what good is living, in a world you never know?

A quote by Theodore Roosevelt comes to mind that pretty much sums up my thoughts about living life.

"Far better it is to dare mighty things, to win glorious triumphs, even though checkered by failure, than to take rank with those poor spirits who neither enjoy much nor suffer much, because they live in the gray twilight that knows not victory nor defeat."

Teddy, I couldn't have said it better myself.

The time is now, and the stage is set, for any free spirit who ever wanted to touch the sky, to climb aboard a real "time machine" and safely experience one of mankind's greatest dreams -- flight.

PARAPLANE PARTS IDENTIFICATION

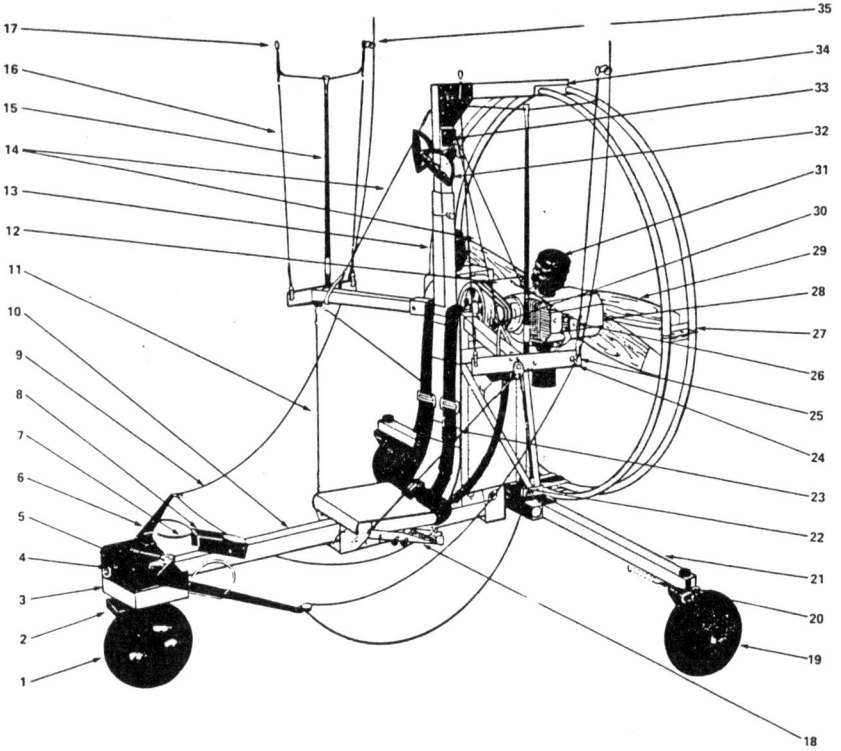

DRAWING COURTESY OF PARAPLANE CORP.

1. NOSE WHEEL — Front wheel turned by the steering levers.

2. WHEEL YOKE — Attaches wheel assembly to the airframe.

3. NOSE SECTION — Houses the Steering mechanisms including the bell crank and steering levers.

4. BELL CRANK — Aids the steering levers in turning the nose wheel.

5. STEERING LEVER GUIDE BRACKET— Houses and establishes the range of motion of the steering lever.

6. STEERING LEVERS — Used for turning the vehicle.

7. STEERING LEVER HEEL LOOPS — Prevents the feet from slipping off the steering levers.

8. MIRROR MOUNT.

9. CANOPY CONTROL LINES — Red lines connected to the canopy and cart which control turning.

10. HORIZONTAL SUPPORT — 1-3/4" sq. main airframe tube that extends from under the seat to the nose section.

11. WEIGHT BEARING CABLES RUNNING FROM THE SUPPORT ARM TO THE MAIN AIRFRAME.

12. COMPRESSION RELEASE CABLES — When pulled, it allows for easier starting of engines.

13. VERTICAL SUPPORT — 1-3/4" sq. main airframe tube that extends behind the seat.

14. STATIC SUPPORT CABLES — Cables which run from the vertical support to the support arms.

15. GUIDE RODS — Swiveling rods attached to the T-Bar which guide the canopy support cables and lines away from the propellers.

16. CANOPY SUPPORT CABLES — Four attachment cables anchored to the T-Bars.

17. CANOPY ATTACHMENT POINT — Canopy connector links attach to these four points.

18. ENGINE CONTROL ASSEMBLY.

19. REAR WHEELS.

20. BUNGEES — Control rear wheel piloting.

21. LANDING GEAR LEGS — Main support for the rear wheels.

22. FUEL TANK — Holds 5 US. gallons.

23. SHOULDER HARNESS AND SEAT BELT — Used to secure the pilot during flight.

24. T-BAR CONTROL LINE GUIDE RING.

25. T-BARS — Mounts for the canopy support cables and guide rods.

26. SPARK PLUGS.

27. PROP GUARDS — Help prevent canopy components from contacting the propellers.

28. COOLING DUCTS — Direct air flow for engine cooling.

29. PROPELLERS.

30. SUPPORT ARMS — Horizontal 1-1/2" sq. tubes extending from the vertical support. They provide spanwise separation for the canopy.

31. EXHAUST MUFFLERS.

32. PULL START GRIPS.

33. STARTER PULLEY BRACKET — Holds the starter pulleys and handles in place.

34. UPPER PROPELLER GUARD ATTACHMENT AND SUPPORT.

35. CONTROL LINE GUIDE RING.

Copies of "The Paraflight Experience" may be ordered directly from Waltz Publishing.

Send check or money order for $14.95 for each book plus $1.75 for postage and handling; with your name and address to:

Waltz Publishing
P. O. Box 6088
Fall River, Mass. 02724

Allow two weeks extra for personal checks.

Back Cover photo of Newport Rhode Island Harbour taken from ParaPlane on 6/29/86 during Tall Ships visit.